The Hiring Network

444 Rules to Live By

by
Susan Orlebeke, SPHR

Information to Encourage Achievement

1261 West Glenlake
Chicago, IL 60660
www.encouragementpress.com

All rights reserved. No part of this book may be reproduced in any form or by any electronic or mechanical means including information storage and retrieval systems or transmitted in whole or in part, in any form or by any means, electronic, mechanical, photocopying, recording or otherwise–except in the case of brief quotations embodied in critical articles or reviews–without prior written permission of Encouragement Press, LLC, Chicago, IL.

Purchasers of this book are granted a license to use the forms contained in this book for their own personal use. No claim of copyright is made to any official government forms reproduced for the benefit or convenience of the reader.

This publication is designed to provide accurate and authoritative information in regard to the subject matter covered. It is sold with the understanding that the publisher is not engaged in rendering legal, accounting or other professional service. If legal advice or other expert assistance is required, the services of a competent professional person should be sought.

From a Declaration of Principles Jointly Adopted by a Committee of the American Bar Association and a Committee of Publishers & Associations.

ISBN-13: 978-1-933766-19-5   ISBN-10: 1-933766-19-0

This product is not intended to provide legal or financial advice or substitute for the advice of an attorney or advisor.

10 9 8 7 6 5 4 3 2 1

©2007 National Institute of Business Management
1750 Old Meadow Road
McClean, VA 22102
www.nibm.net

Introduction, Resources, Index and Appendices
©2007 Encouragement Press, LLC
1261 W. Glenlake
Chicago, IL 60660
www.encouragementpress.com

Special discounts on bulk quantities of Encouragement Press books and products are available to corporations, professional associations and other organizations. For details, contact our Special Sales Department at 1.253.303.0033.

Business Best

The Hiring Network
444 Rule to Live By

About the Author

Some companies just hire people. Smart companies actively recruit and hire producers. Human resources professional, Sue Orlebeke, SPHR provides must follow rules every manager in your company can use to successfully network and recruit the best talent available. With more than 13 years of all-around human resource management experience, Ms. Orlebeke has worked with large and small–from regional and Fortune 500 companies such as Little Caesar Enterprises, University of Chicago Libraries, Au Bon Pain and Cable & Wireless. Ms. Orlebeke earned a B.S. in marketing at Indiana University, Bloomington and the Senior Professional in Human Resources Certification from Society for Human Resource Managers (SHRM). She is also an active affiliate with Children's Oncology Service of Illinois.

Table of Contents

Introduction 1

Chapter 1:
Nonstop Networking 3

Chapter 2:
Secrets of Job Advertising 21

Chapter 3:
Keys to the Hiring Process 29

Chapter 4:
Make Your Company Stand Out 37

Chapter 5:
Online Recruiting 53

Chapter 6:
The Art of Interviewing 77

Chapter 7:
Keep New Recruits on the Job 93

Chapter 8:
Target Special Groups 107

Appendix I
Glossary 133

Appendix II
Best Practices When Hiring New Employees 141

Introduction

WINNING THE WAR FOR TALENT

Employment specialists are warning that despite impressions to the contrary, there is a war for talent, and the war is international in scope. There have been labor shortages in some fields for decades, for example nursing and specialized health care–just to pick one industry. There is every expectation that the need for software engineers, financial services specialists, retail workers and hundreds of other fields will continue unabated for years. What makes the problem particularly acute is that the so-called baby boomers are retiring in droves, creating greater and greater need for qualified, educated and experienced employees. Because of the increasing shortages, some job candidates have more options than ever before–and more leverage in the hiring game. Where does that leave you, the employer?

Your success in recruiting hinges on creating a corporate image that attracts top candidates to your firm by a variety of methods. You need to demonstrate to prospective employees that your company will appreciate them for more than just their professional abilities; you have to show them that it will value–and make room for–their personal lives.

The Nonstop Recruiter: 444 Rules to Live By is just the book to assist all business owners and managers find and recruit the best. In Chapter 1 you will find ways to cast a wide net in the talent pool through continual networking. In Chapter 2 you will learn the most effective ways to advertise for new recruits and in Chapter 3 discover secrets to planning the most productive hiring operation.

Chapter 4 offers tips for making your company stand out in the crowd, while Chapter 5 highlights the newest—and fastest-growing—ways to find new hires: through Internet-based recruiting. Once you have found people to interview, Chapter 6 will show you the best questions to ask and the most effective interviewing techniques.

Make your hiring investment pay off with the ideas in Chapter 7 for keeping new recruits on board. Finally, in Chapter 8, learn ways to mine special groups for job candidates—seniors, people with disabilities, foreign workers, teenagers, college students, Gen-Xers, veterans and welfare recipients.

Remember: Your company is only as good as the people who work there. Be successful in recruiting top talent by staying a step ahead of the competition. It is a time-consuming and exacting process, but a sound investment in hiring will yield a big return for your organization.

Good luck and good recruiting!

Susan Orlebeke, SPHR

Note to our readers:

At the time this book was researched and written, the various strategies for recruiting employees used by individual companies were still in use. Hiring needs and policies change at every company, so certain firms may or may not be using the techniques discussed here. Nevertheless, the ideas presented are sound concepts which may apply to your company and to your recruiting circumstances.

1
Nonstop Networking

The old saying is true:

It is not what you know; it is who you know.

Your ability to network is even more important nowadays since people often do not meet face to face but communicate by email, fax and Websites. The key to successful networking is never to leave any stone unturned. Always ask the people you meet, Do you know anyone else who might be helpful to me?

Says Kathi Jones, HR and recruiting manager for Aventail Corp., a software technology company based in Seattle, "I have been known to network at airports while waiting for a flight–looking for luggage tags with corporate names or reading passengers' company T-shirts and then striking up a conversation. Do not be dashed if the response is, 'Oh, this is my brother's T-shirt.' Say, 'Great! Who is he and what does he do?'"

1 Offer Awards for Employee Referrals

Your own employees can be your best source for new employees. Design an attractive employee referral program, offering incentives and awards for successful hires of referrals. At Deloitte & Touche LLP, the single best source of top talent is the Refer Potential Movers and Shakers program, or RPM, according to Jim Wall, national managing director of human resources, quoted in *Working Woman*.

Here is how it works: Each month, all employees receive an email that lists every job opening, from management to positions in the mail room. Employees who recommend someone who lands a position get $1,500 to $10,000, depending on the job filled. In addition, everyone who successfully refers a candidate is entered into a monthly drawing for a Jeep or a Blazer.

Wall says the RPM program has paid out $3.5 million in cash awards to employees and attracted 1,200 new hires in 1-year alone. That would have cost the firm more than $10 million using traditional methods, such as headhunting and advertising. Another plus: RPM recruits tend to stay longer.

2. Promote Your Referral Program

Enclose fliers with paychecks to remind your employees about the rewards of referring friends and family. And do not wait for employees to come to HR with referrals; regularly hand out updated lists of job openings to everyone. Better yet: Find out when departments gather for monthly or weekly meetings and go in person to deliver your hot jobs sheets.

3. Get Family-Friendly

Send promotional letters to employees' homes outlining the benefits of participation, à la MasterCard. The idea is to get spouses involved in helping refer job candidates. With this and other referral boosters, MasterCard fills 40 percent of its open positions. And do not forget your employees' parents. Southwest Airlines is happy to hire workers' parents. Have you asked your employees to recruit their mom or dad?

4. Be Generous with Referral Bonuses

"Consider how much it costs to recruit someone on the open market, and give generous bonuses to employees who refer a successful job candidate," says consultant Stu Mahlin. "Say you spent $4,000 in ads and successfully recruited four people–that is $1,000 each. Try to match that cost, or at least split the difference, in the bonus you pay to your employees. To motivate your workers even more, pay the bonus in cash and cover taxes."

When the Walt Disney Co. was gearing up for the opening of its newest theme park, California Adventure, it put a bounty on recruits. Current employees get a $50 bonus for referring potential cast members for the new park and a $500 bonus for referring new managers.

5 Match Referral Bonuses to Hard-to-Fill Positions
At the New York-based Internet advertising firm DoubleClick, staffers who persuade a friend to join the company earn $1,000; if the new hire is a computer or Internet technician, the bonus is $5,000.

6 Encourage Employees to Recruit on the Spot
"Give coupons to employees who attend conferences so they can take a new friend to lunch. Encourage employees traveling on business to gather names of new industry acquaintances at seminars, airports or rental car shuttles. And reward them for their efforts," suggests hiring guru John Sullivan, head of the Human Resources Management Program at San Francisco State University, in *Electronic Recruiting Exchange* (ERE.net).

7 Pay Referrals in Installments
Professional Salon Concepts in Joliet, Illinois, doles out rewards in installments for employees who refer job candidates. The firm pays $100 after the new hire has worked 30 days, another $100 after 6 months and $500 on the new employee's 1-year anniversary.

At iXL Enterprises Inc., an Internet consulting company in Atlanta, employees get $3,000 bonuses when a referred candidate stays for at least 90 days. The benefit to employers? Employees recommend only people they believe will stay for the long haul.

8 Look to Your Top Performers
"A players know other A players," says John Sullivan at San Francisco State. So seek referrals especially from your top employees. "Referred candidates are pre-assessed and pre-sold by people who know us well."

9. SET A TIME LIMIT

"Encourage your employees to refer job candidates now by setting a time limit for your employee referral program," consultant Stu Mahlin suggests. "Tie it to a goal. For example, put in a 60-day program before summer or the Christmas shopping season."

10. FOCUS ON YOUR CUSTOMERS

Consider your customers as potential job candidates. Woodcraft Corp., a West Virginia-based firm, needed to replace retiring managers at its Midwest woodworking supply stores. It searched its customer database and mailed several hundred letters soliciting candidates, according to the *Indianapolis Business Journal*. By using its database, the company could mail with precision, targeting those who lived within five miles of a store and who had shopped there within the last year. The bonus: Those people knew the store and had interest in the product.

Instead of the usual help wanted signs posted in windows and on bulletin boards, bagel store chain Einstein Bros. created a job recruitment brochure targeted specifically at customers as job candidates and promoting its casual atmosphere at the same time, according to *The Washington Post*. Chill. Everything's fine, reads the creative flier. You are already coming here, so why not get paid to do it? That simple approach has netted results. Einstein reports that its customer-focused recruiting has helped its stores fill open posts for bagel experts, satisfaction vendors and bagel engineers (i.e., shift leaders, customer service reps and bakers).

11. MAKE IT EASY TO APPLY

Target your customers as potential employees right when they enter your store. In the entryway of Barnes & Noble bookstores customers see posters with this pitch: Now hiring. Apply now. Join the best and brightest book-selling team. In a bin right below the posters are job applications.

Target, the giant retailer, has signs by the checkout counters that advertise openings. Handouts say, For a great job, join our winning team. teamTarget. good pay! a schedule to match yours, benefits you can earn, merchandise discounts....To apply, have a seat in our application kiosk and experience how fast, fun and friendly applying at Target is! Depending on the position and your qualifications, it will take between 5 and 40 minutes.

12 Take a Stab at Direct Mail

It works for products ranging from credit cards to magazine subscriptions. So why not try direct mail when you are looking for employees? Let us say you need high-tech employees. Get subscriber lists to a few high-tech magazines and send out a package that promotes your company and seeks job applicants.

13 Leave Your Calling Card

When the general manager at the Ritz-Carlton in Washington, D.C., gets great service from employees at other businesses, he leaves flattering cards that say, Your service was first class. The cards include his name, number and an offer to interview.

14 Maintain Your Antenna for New Hires

Look around for potential hires for your company. "If I see a good person waiting on me, I'll offer that person a job," says Allen Rifendifer, manager of the Morgan Stewart Gallery at Tanglewood Mall in Roanoke, Virginia. He regularly attempts to recruit workers away from other retailers, particularly local restaurants, he told the *Roanoke Times & World News*.

Whether you have been invited to a sporting event in a luxury box or a PTA meeting, network with others in attendance and steer the conversation to what people do for a living. Chances are they will know someone in your field and maybe that someone will be interested in a new opportunity.

15 Put a Plug in Every Piece of Mail

Use every communication to your customers to solicit job candidates. When J.C. Penney gears up for the Christmas season, it advertises its job openings in millions of national circulars, credit card statements and catalog wrappers.

16 Make Telephone Contact
Follow up on every lead you get. Be direct: Explain the position you are trying to fill and ask if the person is open to hearing more. If you get totally shut down, ask for referrals of friends or colleagues.

17 Use Every Opportunity to Make Your Case
Southwest Airlines recruits with every drink and bag of peanuts handed out. Each passenger gets a napkin with a smiley face made of peanuts and the line: The freedom to be yourself is the freedom to be your best. Check out our great career opportunities at *www.southwest.com*.

18 Use Interviews to Get More Leads
Hiring managers at Dell Computer Corp. constantly fish for talent. During job interviews they always ask, Which boss has had the greatest influence on you? The answer gives them another recruiting lead.

19 Host an Open House
"Invite prequalified candidates to your offices to meet with managers and key team members," hiring guru John Sullivan told *Electronic Recruiting Exchange* (ERE.net). During these open houses, prospects can see first-hand the projects and equipment they would be handling. "The process becomes even more effective when same-day offers and acceptance bonuses are included," he says.

20 Recruit Your Consultants
You already know their work. You already know their personality. If they are a fit, try to hire those who do consulting work for you.

21 Consider Former Employees
When managers are hiring for a specific position at insurance giant Chubb Group, the firm gives them a list of former employees who could fit the bill, *USA Today* reported. The benefit if former employees return? A shortened learning curve because they have already been there, done that.

Three months after employees have left, Deloitte & Touche sends them an anonymous survey asking if they'd consider returning. Recently some 800 to 900 did just that, *USA Today* reported.

Prudential Insurance Co. of America calls departing employees 6 months after they have left to ask what the company could have done to keep them on the job. In some cases, the former employees are even asked if they want their old jobs back.

22 Be Selective with Job Fairs
Cooperative job fairs can be iffy, which is why it is important to do your homework about the quality of prior job fairs or trade shows. Find out more by asking former participants. Make sure participating companies will be seeking to fill similar positions.

For example, if you want a sales manager, you will want to know that other companies there are searching for similar people. Sure, you will have more competition that way, but you will also have more traffic and better-quality applicants.

23 Exhibit at Job Fairs That Highlight Training
Benefit: You will see a broader range of attendees because people who are already employed will have an excuse to be there and will be less fearful of running into their boss or a co-worker.

24 Run Your Own Job Fair
Learn a lesson from a Houston-based energy software firm. When help wanted ads were not bringing results, the 100-employee company began running its own job fairs by renting a hotel conference room and ordering catered food. The events, which cost less than $6,000, are advertised locally and feature quality presentations by company personnel. The firm is able to hire as many as 12 programmers at each event and gets leads on other potential candidates.

25 Open an On-Site Skills Center
Faced with 200 retail stores needing some 4,500 employees, the Jersey Gardens mall in Elizabeth, New Jersey, opened an in-house

skills center that offers basic retail training and applicant screening. Then the recruits are quickly matched with stores in the mall, according to *The Record* in Hackensack, New Jersey.

26. Tap into State Campaigns

Is your state involved in a recruitment campaign to woo back former residents? The Come Home to Minnesota campaign, organized by the state's trade and economic development department, provides employers with online job-board listings, marketing materials, brochures and sample letters they can mail to former residents found through high school reunion lists and college alumni rolls, according to *HR Magazine*.

Michigan Works! distributed an interactive CD-ROM to businesses to hand out to prospective job candidates. The CD-ROM provides employment facts, business trends and lifestyle information.

Bottom line: If you have discounted your state labor department or economic development agency, now is a good time to put their renewed efforts to work for you.

27. Build a Reserve of Former Employees

When an employee resigns, turn the negative into a positive by telling him, "Great! Now you are part of our fluid talent pool," Bruce Tulgan, founder of the training and consulting firm RainmakerThinking Inc., told *Business Week Online*. Ask, "Is there any way that we can keep you involved with some aspect of our work on an ongoing basis? What would you like to work on and when would you like to do it?"

Call, write or email former employees occasionally to see how they are doing, suggests *HRBriefing*. Add their names to your company mailing list so they will get your corporate newsletter or magazine. Some employers try to keep the relationship going even by starting company alumni groups, sponsoring alumni parties and inviting former employees to company events.

28. Tap Departing Employees for Referrals

If an employee has been a valuable asset to your company and the departure is amicable, do not overlook the opportunity to ask for the names of potential candidates. Make it more effective by giving the employee access to recruiting ammunition in the form of printed material about your company. That way, they will be able to sell the benefits you offer when they approach friends about openings at your firm.

29 USE VOICEMAIL JOB HOTLINES

Use a voicemail system as a job hotline. One computer service bureau, for example, established a round-the-clock job hotline, supported by an extensive newspaper ad recruitment campaign. Callers with touch-tone phones can learn about specific types of jobs by punching in the appropriate number (1 for full-time, 2 for part-time and so on) and listening to a recorded listing of available jobs. A second number provides more information about a specific job, and a third number asks the caller to leave a phone number and address for follow-up by a personnel specialist.

30 JOIN FORCES WITH THE ENEMY

If you cannot beat 'em, join 'em. That is the philosophy behind some efforts of competitors to band together to find talent. Instead of raiding your competitor's employee ranks, share resources and try to attract recruits to your corner of the world.

About 50 companies in the greater San Diego area pooled resources to produce a video to help promote their region. The San Diego Regional Recruiting Video, also available on CD-ROM, was shipped to thousands of high-tech workers.

31 MEET AT THE WATERING HOLE

Do not overlook the opportunity to chat up the people around you during happy hour. Bring along a colleague and talk–loudly enough to be overheard without sounding obnoxious–about some of the good things about your firm.

32 TAKE ADVANTAGE OF COMMUNITY EVENTS

When Sun Microsystems Inc. needed engineers for its San Diego office, it went recruiting at the San Diego Marathon. The company had lots of visible advertising and sponsorship materials–and an employment table set up at the event, according to the *Los Angeles Times*.

Sun Microsystems had researched registration data for the marathon and found that 65 percent of the runners were Internet-savvy; the most common occupations were administration and management; and 47 percent earned more than $70,000 a year. Plus, demographically, it knew that athletes are often professionals, well educated and mostly represent passive job seekers, often the hardest to reach.

"If you are going to get to the gainfully employed, you have to jolt them with your message in a place they frequent and where they would not ordinarily see you. It is pretty effective," Dawn Dreyer, who manages recruitment for the firm, told the *Times*.

33 RAID NEARBY EMPLOYERS

If you are targeting recruits from another firm or office park, try this tactic. Go to the restaurant across the street from your target and offer the manager a deal: You will pay for a free dinner for two as the prize for a put-your-business-card-in-the-bowl promotion—as long as the manager shares the business cards with you after the drawing.

34 THINK DEMOGRAPHICS

Tailor recruiting goals to the local population. For example, look for part-timers in a college town, senior citizens near a retirement community and teachers on summer break anywhere.

35 LOOK FOR PUBLISHED EXPERTS

Publish or perish, the saying goes in academia. That may not be the case in corporate America, but there is merit in looking for published experts. Check out publications and Websites in your field, and note the authors of expert pieces. They might be available for part-time, full-time or consulting work.

36 RAISE YOUR PROFILE

Find out what it takes to get on a best places to work list, whether it is a nationwide list, such as *Working Mother's 100 Best Companies,* or similar lists in your local newspaper. You may have to complete a questionnaire or participate in an interview, but that kind of positive exposure is worth all the paid advertising in the world.

If that is a little beyond your reach, speak to local groups, such as the Kiwanis, Optimists or Rotary. Get on a business roundtable. Make presentations at conferences.

37 FIND PRESCREENED SUPPLEMENTAL WORKERS
Draw from a better crop of capable workers with clean backgrounds by letting other employers do the prehire screening for you. Space & Asset Management Inc., a Dayton, Ohio-based office interiors firm, employs off-duty firefighters as supplemental workers to install office furniture for its clients. These workers come with a bonus: Their municipalities have already put them through criminal background checks, basic skills tests, drug tests and more. That translates into both a lower cost per hire and less chance of new-hire failures.

38 MAKE A BID—LITERALLY
Some of your top recruits may be card sharks. Join a bridge or poker game and have your antenna out for the others at the card table. Find out about their current jobs and talk up your company.

39 ENCOURAGE MENTORING OUTSIDE THE COMPANY
Suggest that key employees act as mentors to college students or members of professional associations to which they belong. The people they are mentoring may become likely candidates to join your company. Many companies volunteer in minority areas, helping local high schools develop talented young people.

40 BE GENTLE WITH REJECTIONS
The candidate you reject today could be your new hire tomorrow. With that in mind, be careful when you tell qualified candidates that they did not get the job. Handle these rejections over the phone, keeping the conversation direct and straightforward, suggests *HRBriefing*. Praise their skills and thank them for applying. If possible, refer them to another opening in the company.

41 SCOPE OUT THE COMPETITION
Frequently shop at stores, restaurants or service outlets that are on the same level as your establishment. Scope out the

employees and zero in on those who demonstrate a level of service and professionalism. Then approach them with a pitch: I am impressed by you. Let me tell you what my company can offer you.

42 Use a Recruitment Bus
That is what some school districts do to find bus drivers. They outfit a school bus with interviewers and recruitment materials and drive around town. Use this to complement your print advertising, and stop at advertised, designated spots.

43 Focus on Hiring from Within
Look among your staff for candidates for promotion and lateral moves to fill job openings. As much as 50 percent of an organization's new hires can come from within the company itself.

44 Circulate Fliers
If you are trying to locate sales help, blanket area homes with fliers. Pay a few kids to distribute recruitment fliers door to door.

45 Target Laid-Off Employees
Firms that have to lay off employees often are eager to have recruiters from other companies interview their terminated employees. Unemployed workers are ready to talk and often are willing to relocate for the right job. Watch your business news sections, and quickly notify your HR director of any downsizing firms.

46 Seek Out Graduates of Certificate Programs
"Education and labor trends are combining to encourage growth in specialized certificate programs rather than more traditional education routes," says Roberts Jones, president of the National Alliance of Business in Washington, D.C., in *HRNews*.

47 Recruit Your Sales Reps
Each sales representative or vendor who walks through your door is a potential employee. These people know your firm and know your business. They could be naturals for your firm.

48 Work with Community Groups

Send recruiting fliers to community organizations, neighborhood associations, churches, synagogues, civic groups. Ask them to post your openings on their bulletin boards, announce them at meetings and place notices in their publications and on their Websites.

49 Throw a Recruiting Party

Recruiting parties at techie hangouts are becoming hot events in the swift world of Internet jobs, reports *The Washington Times*. Get Cued Into Your Future, a networking party and job fair sponsored by a radio station and recruiting firm at a billiards cafe in Fairfax, Virginia, attracted some 18 small high-tech firms. To get in the door, job seekers had to have 2 years' experience in information technology and a résumé. Once in, they could play pool all night and drink free beer from 9 to 10 p.m.

Software company Rolu Technologies, in Chantilly, Virginia, held a networking event called Keirets at a coffee lounge. Partygoers were served two free drinks in a take home beer glass emblazoned with the company logo.

AppNet, a Bethesda, Maryland-based Internet firm, held a party at a restaurant/game room and received 500 résumés from people wanting to attend. It extended invitations to 250. After talking jobs, guests could play video games and eat. The result? AppNet conducted 60 follow-up interviews and offered jobs to 20 people.

50 Put Together a Leads Team

Dell Computer Corp. assembles groups of recruiters and employees to gather intelligence to ferret out potential candidates. The groups comb through newspapers, trade journals and company Websites for rising stars, resignations and companies in flux by picking up on mergers, layoffs and declining stock prices, according to *The National Post*.

51 Create a Database of Job Prospects

Keep up with passive job candidates–those who are not searching for a new job right now–with a database tracking system. At Cisco Systems Inc., recruiters have taken a page from the sales staff's handbook and applied it to long-term recruiting: They have created an in-house computer database for tracking job prospects, according to *HRNews*.

Fashioned much like a sales leads database, the company's prospect-tracking system stores information about and records all contact with potential hires—not just with job applicants. The system contains more than 500,000 names and is available to Cisco managers and recruiters at all times from any location.

52 SEND OUT THE BEST

Be aggressive. "Send out the best managers and employees to recruit for you," advises Kevin Wheeler, president of Global Learning Resources Inc., in *Electronic Recruiting Exchange*. "Show off your organization's strengths, and showcase its services and products."

53 HOLD RECRUITER SCHOOL

Take a tip from the U.S. Marine Corps. It sends Marines assigned to recruiting duty to a 2-month recruiter school. They take intensive courses in public relations, speech and sales. Another week of training follows once the Marine reports to a unit, and evaluations follow every 3 months for the next year, according to *Fast Company* magazine.

54 SPONSOR A TEAM

Sponsor a local youth sports team, and put your company's name on every kid's uniform to get your name in front of all those soccer moms and Little League dads in the stands. You never know when one of them could be your next key hire.

FYI: Hiring Time

Are you spending more and more time searching for job candidates? You are not alone. Best estimates now say that it takes an average of 76 days to hire an exempt employee and 45 days to hire a nonexempt employee.

Source: Saratoga Institute, Santa Clara, California.

55 POST OPENINGS ON CONFERENCE MESSAGE BOARDS

You are attending a conference or trade show and right in front of you is a message board that everyone scans. What a perfect place to put your job posting. Include your booth number, cell phone number or hotel phone number so you can arrange interviews on the spot.

56 GO BACK TO SCHOOL

Offer to be a guest lecturer at the local college campus. Colleges often are happy to welcome people from the real world into their classrooms. This can be a good way to get your foot in the door with both students and college faculty. Or consider serving on an advisory board to the college department that studies your industry. Could your company provide a scholarship to a local college? It need not be a major endowment, but it could raise your profile.

57 HAND OUT SPECIAL RECRUITMENT CARDS

Print up business cards with this message on the back: We are always looking for creative people. Interested? Know someone who might be? Please call. Then hand the cards out liberally and leave stacks in strategic areas at meetings and conferences.

58 TAKE YOUR PITCH ON THE ROAD

Sun Microsystems takes its recruitment message on the road, targeting network developers from Seattle to Boston. Dubbed Sun Technology Days, the 2-day event includes a keynote talk by the firm's chief scientist as well as technical and industry lectures, according to *Tech Web*.

59 Check Out Colleges for Teachers

Looking for hard-to-find elementary and secondary math and science teachers? Check your local college or university for retired professors or part-time professors who might be interested in getting back into the classroom. Attend job fairs held for aspiring professors; you may be able to lure some recent grads.

Some progressive firms offer their employees time off for community service or sabbaticals for personal enrichment. You might be able to pick up a math, science or technology teacher from a firm in your own backyard.

60 Cultivate Your Work Force

When an employee goes on vacation, audition a lower-level employee for the job. That is what Arrow Electronics Inc., a Melville, New York-based distributor of electronic components and computer products, does. Instead of having a supervisor or peer do the absent worker's job, Arrow gives the temporary responsibilities to a lower-level employee. Managers then have a chance to gauge leadership potential, company knowledge and work quality.

61 Go to Jail

That is what some employers are doing. Sound crazy? Not to those who have tried it. Faulkner Construction Co. in Austin, Texas, has hired about 150 former inmates since 1992. None has caused a serious problem. Keys to this strategy are careful interviewing, strict rules, training and close supervision. A number of volunteer organizations are working with prisons and former inmates to help them get jobs. Check with local authorities to track down an organization near you.

62 Proactively Headhunt

Rather than wait for experienced people to answer ads, more companies are applying aggressive tactics borrowed from professional headhunters. One approach: Read technical or industry publications with an eye to the credentials of authors and contributors, then call promising prospects and invite them in for an interview.

63 USE YOUR OWN PRODUCT TO RECRUIT

Formerly Bank One Corp. (now Chase) used to put help-wanted ads on ATM screens and deposit receipts. The message reads: Great employment opportunities await you at Bank One. Fax your résumé to . . .

McDonald's prints mini-applications directly on the paper placemats on its food trays, so entry-level prospects can fill in their name, address, phone number and available work hours. A Northeast movie theater pipes its own audio want ads into theater restrooms.

2
Secrets of Job Advertising

Help-wanted ads can be great resources, but like any other tool, you have to know how to get the most out of them. Advertising remains an effective way to recruit top-flight candidates in today's tight labor market. The secret to success in this area: Get their attention early and get it often.

64 DEVELOP A SYSTEM
Each time a job opening occurs, use a specific, written schedule for advertising it and evaluating candidates. Then, stick to your schedule. Do not get buried under the mountain of paper; set up a filing system specifically for résumés, applications and appraisal forms.

65 MAKE YOUR AD COMPELLING
The secret to getting people to respond to your ad is to make it riveting. Make the job sound exciting and show growth potential in the copy. Collaborate with the creative minds in your marketing department to spice up the copy.

66 WRITE A CLEAR AD
You have to grab job candidates quickly—they are not going to spend more than a few seconds on your ad unless there is

something there to pull them in. Mike DeSantis, partner of executive search firm Heidrick & Struggles International of Philadelphia, in a webhire.com article, offers these tips:

- Be clear and concise in your ad.
- Use bullets whenever possible.
- Articulate the mandate of the position; explain where the position fits into the company organization.
- Give an accurate description of the job.
- Describe the position's long-term goals.

67 FIND THE BEST KEY WORD

Most newspapers run help-wanted ads alphabetically according to the first word in the ad. Decide what word that should be. If people are attracted more to your industry than to the specific job opening, you might choose to run your ad under technology or publishing rather than under clerk. If you want a technical person to train as a sales representative, you might want to key the ad engineer or chemist rather than sales.

68 CREATE ATTENTION-GRABBING HEADLINES

Job prospects may never read the body of your ad if you do not write a snazzy headline. Relate the headline to a benefit of the job. For example: Never Dress Up Again! or Earn More Than You Thought Possible!

69 PROMOTE YOUR STRENGTHS

In a tight labor market you have to sell readers on the job, not just announce an opening. Explain what sets your firm apart—whether it is telecommuting or tuition reimbursement. For example, a Booz-Allen & Hamilton ad pictured paper clips, a diaper pin and text about the firm's human side to push its family friendliness.

70 BE CREATIVE IN YOUR JOB TITLES

Draw job candidates to your ad with an attention-grabbing job title. Would you rather be a salesperson or a sales general? A ticket agent or a travel guru?

71 Advertise Community Involvement
Today's job candidates are looking for companies that are community-minded. If you give employees time off for parent-teacher conferences, say so. If you have an employee volunteer program, flaunt it. If you donate a portion of pre-tax profits to charity, say it upfront.

72 Talk Up Wellness Programs
Employees want health club memberships, smoking-cessation programs, health-risk appraisals and wellness materials. Advertise the wellness benefits you offer in your recruiting materials and spell them out during job interviews.

73 Brand Your Company
"Make sure prospects can recognize your company's name, logo or slogan right off the bat," says Carlos Echalar, vice president of human resources at Litton PRC in McLean, Virginia, in a webhire.com article. "When job candidates are already familiar with your company, that cuts down on the selling job your HR department has to do."

"The branding of your company has to complement your HR advertising plan," Echalar says. "Since companies do not want to spend as much on print advertising anymore, they are going to other media—the Internet, radio, TV. It is all about standing out higher than the next company."

74 Convey Your Corporate Culture
Today's job seekers want to know what it feels like at your company. Convey an atmosphere in your ads. Example: Work with top-notch people, face new challenges every day and improve your ping-pong game on the job.

75 Celebrate the Pay
If your pay scale is something to brag about, say so. The Giant Food stores in Maryland place leaflets advertising job openings right on the checkout aisles—with the starting pay in boldface.

76 Advertise the Fun

Today's younger workers want a corporate culture that is fun, a place where they can hang out while working. Feature your environment in your ads, whether it is a Lego room, a sliding board to get downstairs, a weekly party or a company softball team.

77 Flaunt Employee Discounts

Can your company offer any employee discounts? Few firms that do this actually mention the policy in their help-wanted advertising. Those that do, however, say it is an attractive lure–so attractive, in fact, that some have expanded their discount programs to include part-time employees.

78 Tout Your Benefits

Be sure to mention company benefits in your ad, especially any unusual ones that could give you a competitive edge. Do you offer health club memberships, tuition reimbursement, elder care referral or concierge services? If you do, say so. It is particularly important to advertise your benefits if they are better than your competitors'.

79 Promote Your Firm

Sell job prospects on your company, not just on the specific opening. Is your firm a leader in its field? Is the field itself a growth industry? Has your company won any awards? Is it considered a best place to work?

80 Target Your Audience

Looking for teenage workers? Follow the lead of Dierberg's Markets in Chesterfield, Missouri, which runs help-wanted ads in high school and college newspapers. Even better: It lists employment opportunities in driver's education notebooks used in area high schools.

81 Qualify Candidates Right Off the Bat

Ask for more than a résumé. Suggests POWERHiring.com: At the end of your ad, ask the candidate to submit a one-page write-up of their most significant comparable accomplishment. The quality of the accomplishment is more predictive of success than all the degrees and experiences in the world.

82 TRY YOUR AD IN OTHER NEWSPAPER SECTIONS
Some firms have great success placing display ads in, say, the sports or food sections. Those sections have high readership and will attract candidates who are thinking about, but not pursuing, a job change. A sporting goods store in Oregon put its help-wanted ads in the sports section, not in the classifieds.

83 CROSS-REFERENCE ADS
To attract the largest possible number of prospects, consider running two ads and cross-reference them. For example, under publishing, say see our ad under clerk-typist.

84 DO NOT NEGLECT THE SUNDAY PAPER
The Sunday paper is still the king of employment ads. Your ads get the most readership that day, even though an all-week campaign is a good idea because the applicant you are seeking could be looking for a job on any given day of the week.

85 RUN YOUR AD SEVERAL CONSECUTIVE DAYS
Running your ad 4 to 7 days is generally recommended. The more experience or expertise required in the job, the longer you will need to run the ad.

86 ADVERTISE IN TRADE JOURNALS
That is where you will find self-selected prospects who are already interested in your field. Keep your company's name before your public with regular ads in trade or industry magazines, newspapers, journals and newsletters.

87 USE CONFERENCE BOOTHS
"Post a strong recruiting message on the booths you set up at trade shows or industry conferences," advises Mark S.A. Smith, a

Boulder, Colorado-based trainer, consultant and author. "After all, you know those walking the exhibit hall have some kind of interest in your product or service, simply by virtue of their attendance."

Just as important, think about whom you are going to send to the next industry conference. Your employees will be walking those exhibit halls and could be taken in by your competitor's job pitch.

88 DO NOT UNDERRATE TV
The Elkhart County, Indiana, government solicits job applicants with a 30-second TV commercial touting the benefits of working in the public sector. The ad cost about $600 to produce and the airtime cost $3,000, according to the *South Bend Tribune*. So far, the investment has paid off–with a fourfold rise in job applications.

89 REMEMBER RADIO, TOO
Especially in large markets, radio station ads appeal to narrow demographic segments. If you want to appeal to teens, try the hot new station that kids listen to. Or, use radio to refer listeners to your newspaper ads to heighten response.

90 PAINT A BILLBOARD
Make a bold statement by bringing your recruitment campaign to highway billboards. Some companies put their billboard job ads on the roads leading in and out of major city airports to attract the attention of business travelers.

91 HANG OVERSIZE SIGNS
Hang huge recruitment banners on the outside of your office building or store. Be sure to include a phone number or Website address to contact.

92 ADVERTISE ON BUSES, SUBWAYS
Put your recruitment pitch right in the face of commuters. Include your company slogan, an easy phone number to call or a Website to visit.

93 Use Moving Ads
Do as the Walt Disney Co. does, and make your ads a moving target. Disney staff use moving advertisements: Driving around Orlando in painted vans that display a toll-free Disney jobs hotline.

94 Do Not Forget About the Locals
Those free community newspapers delivered to your neighbors' doors are well-read publications. Do not overlook their classified sections; they are a great place for listing your recruitment ads.

95 Go to the Movies
Filmgoers used to watch short subjects and previews while munching popcorn and waiting for the movie to start. Now that the big screen is filled with ads before the feature presentation, take advantage of it. Put job recruitment ads for your firm in the local theaters. Hint: Capitalize on the setting by tying some movie trivia into your recruitment pitch.

96 Use an Ad Agency
If you have access to an advertising agency, ask for advice. The firm's copywriters may be able to offer some innovative and inexpensive ideas that could help improve your search.

97 Consider Hiring a Ghostwriter
Some firms do nothing but create and place employment ads–and they know what works. Two of the largest: Nationwide Advertising Services in Cleveland, 800.627.4723, and Bernard Hodes Advertising Inc., 888.438.9911.

98 Do Not Settle for a Half-Baked Mailer
If you are recruiting through direct mail, be professional–get your mailer done by an expert. After all, you do not hire a plumber to take out your gallbladder or let the sales manager play direct-mail copy maven. Invest a little money to hire a pro. Also, address the envelopes personally if possible and mail them first-class.

3
Keys to the Hiring Process

Your hiring process should be part of your overall strategy for corporate growth. Hiring is a complicated business—one that begins with an initial contact and does not end until your recruit signs on the bottom line. But in today's society speed counts, so do not hesitate if you have got a live one on the line.

99 PUT YOUR BEST FOOT FORWARD
Make sure your best people are doing the hiring. In the Marines, only the top 10 percent of the corps gets a shot at recruitment duty, according to *Fast Company* magazine. "Recruiting is all about creating a clear picture of your organization. The best way to do that is to put the best product of that organization in front of potential recruits," a Marine recruiter said.

100 ACCELERATE THE PROCESS
Today's job candidates are impatient. More than a few employers have even found their hot prospects accepting job offers and then backing out or not showing up for the first day of work, a survey by *Executive Recruiter News* found. Try these tactics:

- Keep the time short between when you offer a job and the start date of employment.
- Make the evaluation process as fast as possible.
- Negotiate the offer quickly and be competitive upfront. Avoid going back and forth for just a little movement up or down.
- Consider signing bonuses for particularly hard-to-fill jobs.
- Finally, do not announce that the job is filled until the person begins work.

101 Respond within 24 Hours

Hiring guru Lou Adler says it is crucial to "Express your interest and get the process started within 24 hours of getting an online résumé. You can use an auto-response email, but be sure to make it sound personal and heartfelt," he says in *Hireadigm: Recruiting News for Professionals*. Adler suggests you say: "Thanks for sending in your résumé. You have got an impressive background. We will be back in touch with you very shortly."

102 Set Up Interviews within 72 Hours

Phone your top candidates within 72 hours to set up interviews. The goal? To hold the interview within 5 days. Try to follow that by an offer and hire within 2 weeks.

103 Focus on Their Message, Not Yours

"When recruiting, right from the first call to the candidates, it is all about them," says a HR manager at Aventail Corp. "There is no song and dance about us. Rather, we start by asking them what they want and then assess whether and how we can offer that. We get their message upfront, rather than giving our own."

104 Map Out Employee-Success Profiles

To avoid new-hire mismatches, write employee-success profiles that define the ideal fit before you begin screening candidates. The idea is to identify the traits, behaviors and attitudes that are necessary to succeed at the company. Think of it as a way to expand your basic job description. Bottom line: Develop an ideal employee profile and hiring managers will know exactly what they are seeking.

105 IDENTIFY THE RIGHT HIRING STRATEGY
Who are your most successful recruits? At GE Medical Systems, just 1 percent of the people who send in résumés get interviews, but 10 percent of employee referrals nail down an interview and a hire, reports *Fortune*. Result: The firm aggressively courts employee referrals through a generous bonus program.

106 ACCELERATE THE OFFER PROCESS
Digital Island, a San Francisco-based firm, has job offers on prospects' voice mails by the time they drive home from their interview. "Our approach is speed, rather than courtship. We recognize the candidate we want and give them an offer very quickly," says company staffing manager Margaret Gillette. "Speed has been far more effective than wining or dining," she says in a CMP Media Inc. article on webhire.com.

107 GRADE EACH RÉSUMÉ
Like Zagat does in its restaurant guides, create numerical grades to get a quick scan of the most promising candidates. Example: Take every qualifying résumé and rate it on a scale of 1 to 10 for depth of experience, education and the relevance of affiliations and activities. Use a preprinted form or computer spreadsheet. Establish a perfect 10 for every job to apply a fair basis of comparison.

108 MATCH COMPETENCIES
List up to 14 well-defined skills that the position requires. Then use the résumé, application and phone interview to rate how closely candidates meet the criteria. Prompt them to discuss those areas where they may lack key competencies, and let them commit to gaining new skills or modifying existing skills to fit your needs.

Speed Is Everything

"A fast hiring process is your best recruiting weapon," says David Sikora, president of PeopleSense.Inc., in *Hireadigm: Recruiting News for Professionals*. Sikora offers these tips:

- **Have a recruiting plan.**
  Define your target candidates, identify ways to reach them and lay out your firm's unique hiring advantages.

- **Stay in hiring mode all the time.**
  Be ready to interview and hire when-ever you find good candidates. "Organizations committed to improvement always find room for great employees."

- **Keep a list of targeted candidates.**
  Be a talent scout. Keep a list of people you would like to hire.

- **Have recruiting materials ready.**
  Always have available recruiting brochures, company overviews, job applications and information about your benefits.

- **Keep your process simple.**
  Involve only a few employees in the interview process, and stay involved yourself. That saves time because you do not have to bring candidates back a second time.

- **Set tight deadlines for each step of your hiring process.**
  Set the parameters of your interviewing and hiring process. Move from one step to the next within 1 business day.

- **Keep your process flexible.**
  Meet candidates when and where they are available, even if this means before- or after-hours interviews or going to their location. "And whenever you are faced with a potentially time-consuming roadblock, think speed and creativity."

- **Make fast hiring decisions.**
  Meet quickly with anyone involved in the process. Make a decision within an hour of the interview. "Better yet, while someone is taking your candidate on a tour, or taking them out to lunch, gather the interviewers. Make a decision before the candidate returns."

- **Use interviewing teams.**
  If it is necessary for a few people to interview a prospect, have those people participate in each interview, rather than spread out several interviews over several days. "It is faster than a protracted series of one-on-one discussions, and the candidate will see that you do things in creative, nontraditional ways."

- **Go online.**
  Encourage prospects to email their résumés to you and think about advertising jobs online. Also, look into online background and reference-checking services. "These Internet-based companies can generally turn around information in hours or days, rather than weeks."

109 Track How You Find Your Best Hires
Aside from referrals, weigh your results using interns, temps and professional recruiters. With each method, measure first-pass yield (the percentage of résumés that result in interviews) and second-pass yield (the percentage of interviews that lead to offers).

110 Involve Your CEO
"The CEO has to have an active role in how the organization presents itself to candidates," according to Ronald D. Raab, CEO of RD Raab & Co., a Philadelphia recruiting and staffing firm. "It is important for the top exec to be involved in the hiring process, rather than leave it entirely to the HR director."

111 Hire for Talent; Train for Skills
In today's market, the ideal candidate for many organizations is someone 80 percent—not 100 percent—ready for the job, according to *Employment Trends Outlook*. The prevailing view: Acknowledge that finding perfect fits will be tough to do repeatedly. Select candidates who are largely suited for the job but who are also amenable to change, flexibility and growth.

112 Give Them a Tryout
Consider giving job candidates a tryout on the job before offering them a permanent position. In fact, a real-life tryout—one that exposes them to the most critical functions of the position—can predict 44 percent of likely performance. By contrast, conducting a structured interview predicts just 21 percent of performance traits, according to *Workforce Stability Alert*.

Headhunter listings

For listings of headhunters, check out the *Directory of Executive Recruiters* from Kennedy Publications, 800.531.0007, or *The Euro Directory: Executive Search and Selection Firms in Europe* from *The Recruiting and Search Report*, 800.634.4548.

Contingency search firms generally specialize in either professional/technical or administrative applicants and are paid only if they find a suitable candidate whom you hire. To find a contingency search firm with professional industry certification, check out *The National Directory of Personnel Services*, published by the National Association of Personnel Services in Alexandria, Virginia.

113 HIRE A SEARCH FIRM

When the going gets tough, consider using a professional search firm. Search firms often work with senior-level executives in the salary range of $60,000–$200,000 and up in a wide range of industries and functions.

Executive recruiters say searching is easier now that résumés are entered into databases, allowing them to enter the qualifications required–including experience, geography and education–and pull up a list of viable candidates from literally thousands of résumés.

114 NEGOTIATE FEES

Seek flexible pricing options when you negotiate fees and rates with executive search firms. You can take advantage of the fact that search firms know they have to be more competitive today to get your business.

115 SHOP FOR THE BEST

Korn/Ferry International suggests that you ask the following questions when shopping for an executive search firm:

- Will the consultant be a credible ambassador for your organization?
- Does the consultant understand your organization and its environment?
- Does the consultant have the right experience to handle your assignments?
- Will the consultant give you top priority?
- Will the firm's best people handle the assignment?
- Are you comfortable with the consultant's approach and do you feel the assignment will be handled effectively?

Make Your Company Stand Out
4

Some may think they are gimmicks. Others might consider them perks. But whatever you can do to distinguish your company from the competition will help you win the War For Talent. The possibilities are endless.

116 **OFFER ENTERTAINMENT FREEBIES**
To lure tech workers, Datatel Inc. of Virginia gives all its employees a $75 annual entertainment reimbursement. Plus, they get to choose a pair of tickets to a concert or sporting event a few times a year.

117 **ADD A BMW TO THE MIX**
One company in Georgia offered a BMW as an incentive for job candidates to sign on with the firm. Not a bad deal!

118 **GIVE THEM A BUTLER**
In today's fast-paced, stressed-out world, employees are looking for anything that will make their lives easier. Concierge services, such as prepared take-home meals, dry cleaning pickup, bill paying, hotel reservations, counseling or babysitting, are now offered by 26 of Fortune's 100 Best Places to Work, up from 15 companies 2 years ago.

119 Promote Individualism

MentalPhysics Inc., an Internet firm based in Arlington, Virginia, promotes individualism. Employees get to create their own, one-of-a-kind desks by choosing the door they want from Home Depot, table legs from IKEA and any color of paint, *The Washington Post* reports. The result: Employees' personalities come to life at the office, and the company's founders have noticed an uptick in employee referrals and job inquiries.

120 Talk to Spouses

When recruiting employees, Dell Computer spends time talking to the candidates' spouses. Dell staffers show spouses area schools, match up their children with team coaches... In essence, they do whatever it takes to sell the virtues of work and life around Dell.

121 Develop Work/Life Plans

Helping employees balance their work and home lives is more important than ever. Make your firm stand out in this area to attract the best and the brightest. Phoenix Home Life put together a formal work/life strategy after executives realized the perks could be used to recruit new hires and retain current workers.

The firm's program has four key areas:

1. Maintain a flexible workplace, including alternative work schedules, job sharing and permanent part-time positions.
2. Meet the needs of time-deprived employees with an on-site medical clinic, financial workshops and convenience services.
3. Allow employees to do volunteer work on company time.
4. Focus on low-cost, innovative programs, such as an adoption fair and homework hotline.

The result? Job openings are down by 30 percent and 90 percent of women returning from maternity leave stay on the job.

122 Find Your Unique Selling Point
Not every business is located in San Francisco, New York City or Lake Tahoe. If you are in a hard-to-sell area, flaunt your advantages. Are there lots of young people? Nearby weekend getaways? Low housing costs? Beautiful scenery? A small Texas school district uses this pitch: Our kids are polite, you will not sit in traffic and we are only an hour from Houston.

123 Dangle a Carrot to Temps
Encourage temporary workers to apply for a permanent job by paying them a little less when they are temporary than they would make if they came on board. That gives them an incentive to secure a regular, salaried position.

124 Conduct Mini Tryouts
When hiring for hourly jobs, a supervisor should work with prospective employees for 3 or 4 hours "to get a feel for how they do under game conditions," advises author Pierre Mornell. That way, you can make your decision based on performance.

That is exactly what a franchisee of Cookies By Design in San Diego does. As part of the interview process, applicants take orders, decorate cookies and assemble bouquets for an hour or so, according to *Nation's Business*. "You can tell if a person is going to have the knack or not," the franchisee was quoted as saying. The result? Employees are better matches for the job and tend to stay on longer.

125 Send Interns on Business Trips
Give your college interns a taste of life in the fast lane. Goldman Sachs, the New York-based investment banking house, sends its summer interns on business trips with the firm's associates. Along with the clients, the interns are wined and dined.

Make Your Company Stand Out

126 Get Down on Your Knees
At a San Jose-based start-up used a marriage proposal to recruit a key employee. The chief technology officer of the e-business company got down on one knee to marry the vice president of marketing to recruit her to the company–the idea being they would prosper together.

127 Feed Them
Reel in job prospects with the promise of food perks. Subsidized meals, delivery and on-site food preparation are timesavers for employees–especially during hectic seasonal crunch times, according to *The Denver Post*.

Catalog retailer Professional Cutlery Direct LLC, of North Branford, Connecticut, employs a professional chef to answer customers' questions. In his spare time, the chef cooks for the company staff–a nice perk that they appreciate during the busy holiday season, when lunch breaks are scarce.

Scott's Liquid Gold, a Denver-based manufacturer, hires its own cooks and runs a small, on-site cafeteria independently, picking up a large portion of the meal tab for workers.

128 Bond Them with a Trip
Entice new hires with a new-to-the-job bonding experience. Janus, the Denver-based money fund, takes its batch of top new college recruits on an outdoor adventure trip a week after they begin in August.

129 Try Low-Cost Wellness Programs
Health promotion perks are a cost-saving recruitment tactic. Easy offerings include flu shots, health fairs, seminars and health appraisals.

130 Help Spouses with Job Search
Offering job-search help for spouses of workers you are recruiting can be an extra incentive to cement a job offer. In Ohio several high-tech firms banded together in a network to share job openings for the displaced spouses of senior-level new hires.

The Hiring Network: 444 Rules to Live By

131 Offer Midweek Weekends
Do you run a 7-day-a-week operation? Could your employees perform their jobs any days of the week if they wanted? If the answer to either question is yes, offer employees their choice of when to take their weekend. Job recruits will be happy to know they have the option of taking their days off when malls and exercise facilities are less crowded.

132 Reel Them in with a Hiring Bonus
A survey by Buck Consultants reported that 76 percent of Fortune 1000 employers used hiring bonuses to attract employees and 50 percent used retention bonuses for existing staff. Some hospitals are offering as much as $5,000 in signing bonuses to nurses, given the grave nursing shortages they face.

133 Move Them with a Pro
When recruiting out-of-area employees, offer them the services of a real estate agent. Not only can the agent help them find a house, but an agent has a wealth of information on neighborhoods, schools, shopping and community groups.

134 Encourage Volunteerism
Potential job candidates view the organization as a good place to work when you encourage community service. Job candidates swarmed a Habitat for Humanity site when an accounting firm in Los Angeles invited them to pitch in for 8 hours to build houses for the poor.

Nearly half of Deloitte & Touche's 1,200 Chicago employees volunteer either on company time or on their own. Fannie Mae grants employees 10 hours of paid leave a month for volunteer work and matches the volunteer hours of an employee with grants from the company's foundation.

135 Keep Health Benefits Front and Center
Despite all the new-line benefits, the traditional one—health benefits—remains crucial to accepting a job. Three-quarters of 1,028 workers surveyed by Consortium Health plans, an alliance of 16

Make Your Company Stand Out

Blue Cross/Blue Shield providers, say health insurance benefits are key to taking a job.

136 Take It to the Max
Rent or buy a place in the mountains or on the beach, and entice recruits with the promise of its availability to every staff member at least once a year.

137 Reward Boomerangs
Many employees of Gensler, a San Francisco-based international architectural design firm, proudly display boomerangs in their offices. The reason: Former employees often decide to come back to the firm. The boomerang program has helped the firm attain a return rate of 12 percent, one of the highest in the profession.

138 Be Generous with Time Off
Start work any time at Capitol One, a Virginia-based financial services company and the next year you get 3 full weeks of vacation. Plus, employees have the option to buy a 4th week. They get 3 family care days to use for sick children, field trips, elder care needs and so forth; emergency vacation days, available at 30 minutes' notice, can be taken from the 3-week vacation. Those policies complement generous work/family benefits, tuition reimbursement and education leave.

"We are a rapidly growing company," says the senior vice president for human resources. "To do that, we adopted the philosophy that we have to design our product offering—that product being our benefits package and compensation—around what it takes to recruit and retain talented people."

139 Have the CEO Make a Pitch
Have your CEO visit or call your top job candidates. "The recruiting tool that has the highest success rate (it is 100 percent at some firms) is having the CEO personally ask the recruit to join the firm," says hiring expert John Sullivan in *Electronic Recruiting Exchange*. "Bill Gates has been known to do it and every top recruiter that I have ever asked

about it responds almost immediately with the same mantra, It works every time!" The reasons:

- Just knowing that the CEO knows who you are is a WOW just by itself.
- The candidate has a story to tell family and friends–this is especially good for college hires.
- Once the CEO calls, candidates feel bound to have influence and access if they take the offer.
- The shock value makes your job offer stand out.
- CEOs are usually very convincing individuals and make a great recruiting pitch.

"To make this tactic most effective, the CEO should make a pitch about the person's importance to the company and infer that he will work closely with the candidates. The CEO should ask for a yes immediately and should show excitement and enthusiasm on the spot," Sullivan says. "Finally, where appropriate, the CEO should call the spouse to welcome him or her aboard."

140 Sub in a Senior Manager

"If the CEO is not available to contact a recruit, a visit or phone call from a senior vice president or top manager can also be effective," John Sullivan says.

141 Supply a Free PC

Entice recruits with the promise of a free PC. Ford Motor Co. started the trend when it announced it would give its more than 101,000 U.S. workers personal computers, printers and discounted Internet service. A day later, Delta Air Lines followed suit for its 80,000 employees and then Intel chipped in. Intel is giving 70,000 full- and part-time employees computers and Internet service, with regular, free upgrades.

142 Offer a Choice in Health Benefits

Job candidates want a choice of health insurance plans. In a recent survey, four of five employees said that choice was important to them. Shop with several health care plans to find out your options.

Make Your Company Stand Out

143 Broaden the Potential for Flextime

When pharmaceutical giant Merck Co. posts job openings in-house, its managers list all types of flexible work arrangements they would consider. That way, employees know upfront that flexible arrangements are possible–but they also know the extent of the flexibility.

144 Brew Another Perk

Job candidates will smell the freshly brewed java when they come in for their interview. Tell them about the specialty blends brewed in the office each morning, and they will know they could get their day off to a good start in your firm. Yarde Metals, a Bristol, Connecticut wholesale metal distributor, has fresh brew shuttled to each of the company's branches every day.

145 Offer Employee Discounts

If you are a retail, wholesale or service business, give your employees discounts on your products and services.

146 Attract the Sports Fans

Buy season tickets to your local sports franchise, whether it is the Yankees or an AAA minor-league team. Let recruits know that tickets are available to everyone.

147 Let Them Breathe Mountain Air

Is your firm located in the city and your perfect recruit lives in the mountains? If that is a stumbling block, let her work from there. Offer her a home office setup (if she does not have one already) and plane fare to your offices for monthly status meetings.

148 Give Freebies

Let job candidates know they will benefit by getting freebies from the job. Ben & Jerry's, the ice cream manufacturer, gives employees at its Vermont plant free pints to take home every day.

149 Throw a Party

Host a barbecue for job recruits at an associate's house or have a dinner party in a local restaurant. This gives you a chance to see job candidates in an informal social setting and lets them see how people in your firm have fun.

150 Use Web Service for Expatriates

Do you need executives to send abroad for short- or long-term assignments? Check out expatriates.com, an Internet-based service designed to make expatriate assignments more successful. It has three major components: preparation for the nuts and bolts of daily life; selection of neighborhood and housing; and exploring opportunities for expat spouses, significant others and family members. Visit *www.expatriates.com*.

151 Take Advantage of Your Buying Power

Try to attain discounts for your employees from local or national vendors. Employeesavings.com helps you attract and retain employees by offering discounts, usually of 5 percent to 10 percent, on products and services ranging from groceries, golf clubs and sporting events to cars, homes and travel. Employees can access the discounts through custom Websites designed for their employer, through print catalogs or by using a discount card in person at retailers. Participating employers pay nothing. The Bellevue, Washington-based firm's revenues come from the companies that offer their products and services. Call 877.327.8483 or go to *www.employeesavings.com*.

152 Pay Attention to Work/Life Benefits

"While candidates care deeply about compensation, work/life benefits often are the deciding factor in accepting an offer," says Cecil Gregg, executive director of RHI Management Resources. "Companies are recognizing that these programs are critical in recruiting the best talent."

"Benefits such as telecommuting, flextime and subsidized day care help reduce the pressure of long work hours," Gregg says. An RHI survey of 1,400 CFOs from companies with more than 20 employees found that 63 percent had more work/life benefits than they did 5 years ago.

153 Offer a Choice of Rewards

Brian Loew, former CEO of Worldweb.net in Alexandria, Virginia believes in the power of choice. His tactic: Besides giving employees $2,500 for referrals who are hired, Loew gives his staff a choice of two of the following perks:

- A wireless phone and monthly access.
- Broadband Internet access at home.
- Free parking.
- A month's subscription to an online grocery store.
- Regular car washes.
- A health club membership.

154 Buy Tickets to Cultural Events

Does your area have a symphony orchestra or a local playhouse? Either way, pick up tickets to a variety of events, and make them available to employees.

155 Make Yourself Unique

Put on your thinking cap to tap into something proprietary, special, unusual and fun to offer employees. Find that special thing that will stand out as a one-of-a-kind benefit of working at your company.

156 Encourage Humor

A William M. Mercer Inc. survey of employers found 62 percent believe that encouraging fun or humor in the workplace helps employees and the organization as a whole and aids in attracting and keeping employees. Many companies said they encourage togetherness as a way to promote fun. Examples: birthdays and other personal celebrations, social events, employee sports teams and business celebrations for making major sales.

157 Help with Bill-Paying Service
Offer a bill-paying service to help employees save time and money. Paytrust is an online bill management service. Employees have their bills sent to the Paytrust and the service notifies them via email when bills arrive. Employees then log into their secure account and give instructions on when and how much to pay on each bill.

158 Keep New Moms on the Job
Offer a formal lactation program for new mothers returning to the workplace. Wells Fargo, the San Francisco-based bank, provides for new moms a private space, a hospital-quality breast pump, a refrigerator where they can store bottles of milk, as well as a consultant to answer questions. Wells Fargo says new mothers come back to work an average of 4 to 6 weeks earlier than they did before the program began.

159 Clean up Your Act
Office space that looks cluttered, old or disorganized is a drag on recruiting. In fact, in a survey of managers by research firm HLW International, 38 percent said unkempt offices hurt recruiting and 40 percent said the mess has a negative effect on retention.

What do employees want? Work space conducive to productivity and creativity—not antiseptically neat but not overly sloppy, either.

160 Pay Attention to Elder Care Concerns
Employees who care for elder relatives will appreciate anything you can do to lighten their burden. Try offering coordinated elder care services through SeniorAdvocate. The service, offered by ARAG Group of Des Moines, Iowa, provides affordable access to attorneys, financial and tax counselors and elder care specialists. Employers can either sponsor or pay for the benefit. Contact ARAG at 800.888.4184.

To find free or low-cost help from nonprofit agencies, governments and volunteer groups, log onto *www.elderweb.com*, or contact your local agency on aging.

161 Let Employees Buy and Sell Vacation Days
With this benefit, employees can exert more control over their own schedules. Workers at 7-Eleven can sell their vacation leave via an automated telephone system.

162 Keep Your Reputation Top-Notch
"Perception is everything in attracting top talent," says Christopher Komisarjevsky, former CEO of Burson-Marsteller and Wirthlin Worldwide. Overall, a company's reputation is more important today than it was 5 years ago, according to a Burson-Marsteller study of Fortune 500 companies. In fact, respondents reported that firms with great reputations are four times more likely to be recommended as a good place to work. When asked who has the most influence on a company's reputation, customers and employees led the list, followed by the media, the public, the CEO and the community at large.

163 Match Life Interests
Harvard Business School psychologists tout the importance of matching jobs to workers' deeply imbedded life interests. These are not hobbies; they are passions. Life interests trump ability and rewards when it comes to being satisfied with your career. In Harvard Business Review, the researchers focus on how managers can avoid losing good employees by sculpting jobs to suit their interests.

164 Tap into Stay-at-Home Moms
Many stay-at-home mothers would like to work; they just do not want to work full-time. Sunrise Assisted Living Inc., based in McLean, Virginia is going out of its way to lure these mothers to work with the offer of two-thirds-time jobs. "You get close to 100 percent work out of an 80-percent person," Paul Klaasdan, chief executive of the chain of senior care facilities, told *The Washington Times*. The firm seeks women who have cared for children and elderly parents at home because those skills translate to caring for elderly residents of Sunrise's assisted- and independent-living facilities.

165 Try Out Telecommuting

More and more employees want to work from home, whether for family reasons or to cut down on commuting time. Entice these candidates to your firm by offering telecommuting options. There are many ways to set this up, from full-time telecommuting to working at home 1 or 2 days a week.

And if you are worried about the outcome, consider this: Research consistently shows increased productivity and job satisfaction among telecommuters.

166 Hire a Decorator for Employees

Each new employee at Richmond, Virginia-based Xperts Inc. gets the services of a professional interior decorator to make his own work space as personal and comfortable as possible. The results make for an interesting collection of tastes—and they show off the firm's focus on individuality to new recruits. One employee decorated her office in a beach theme; another displayed his love of golf; a military buff added a full suit of armor to stand guard at his office door.

"We've already spent $3,000 on a computer for each employee, so why not spend $1,500 more and let them have a consultation with an interior decorator," CEO William Tyler told *Virginia Business*. The firm gets a steady dose of valuable employee referrals and turnover has decreased. Says Tyler: "So I provide the positive environment; they bring the positive attitude."

167 Showcase Your Benefits

Highlight your benefits package in high-traffic areas where employees gather or walk by every day. Job prospects coming in for interviews or touring your offices will see that you give these programs a high profile. In addition to the usual posters and fliers, display recent articles or testimonials about your benefits package.

168 Make It Personal

Gearworks.com of Northfield, Minnesota was recruiting a candidate from a warmer climate who was not sure about moving to Minnesota, according to a CMP Media Inc. article on webhire.com. What did the mobile Internet applications provider do?

Along with his airline ticket for his interview, they sent him long underwear. The prospect took the job.

Stability Is Still Key

Other than salary and traditional benefits, the stability and reputation of a company are the top considerations in accepting a job offer, a survey of chief financial officers shows. Developed by RHI Management Resources, the survey asked CFOs this question: "Other than salary and traditional benefits such as health insurance and 401(k)s, which of the following, in your opinion, is the most appealing to senior-level executives when considering an employment offer?"

The results:

- Stability of the company/company reputation — 44 percent
- Work/life balance program — 22 percent
- Stock options — 18 percent
- The challenge/prestige of position — 13 percent
- Other — 1 percent
- Do not know/no answer — 2 percent

"Established companies with sustainable growth and a solid reputation are often viewed as providing the best job security," says Cecil Gregg, fomer executive director at RHI. "While the opportunity and challenge of working for high-tech start-ups appeals to many executives, the potential for long-term career satisfaction and work/life balance with a reputable firm that has a proven track record is still an attractivr incentive to professionals at this level."

169 Sponsor a Contest

The lengths to which recruiters will go to attract workers in this job market seem to have no bounds. A recent strategy: The Promote Yourself Career Contest, sponsored by Enterprise Rent-A-Car. The contest featured cash prizes of $1,000 to $5,000 and job offers to qualified business management career candidates who produced unique and nontraditional résumés.

Grand prize went to the person who submitted a game board with dice, Matchbox car tokens and résumé playing cards. Second place was a home video stand-up résumé routine. There were three third-place winners: an

Austin Powers video spoof shot at locations detailed in a résumé; a man's shoe, to get a foot in the door, with a slick CD-ROM résumé; and a large super-résumé pizza box with precut slices of pepperoni.

Not only did the contest succeed in calling attention to opportunities in Enterprise's business management program, but it produced a bumper crop of résumés.

170 MAKE RELOCATION A BREEZE

Arm yourself with a list of ways to help job candidates relocate to take your job. Here are tips from the Metropolitan Washington Work/Life Coalition:

- Help them find and finance affordable housing.
- Reimburse for house-hunting trips.
- Pay for temporary hotel housing.
- Offer to help the employee's spouse find a job.
- Provide child and elder care resources.
- Offer information about schools, hospitals, churches and veterinarians.

If families are moving to another country, offer language lessons and assistance in adapting to the new culture.

171 DO A SEASONAL SWAP

Here is an unusual but successful recruitment team effort between hospitals in the Sun Belt and Snow Belt. A Florida facility was bursting at the seams in the winter because of visitors from the North, while a Minnesota hospital experienced opposite seasonal variations. The hospitals arranged for housing and staff rotation to allow a few nurses to spend their winters working in Florida and their summers in Minnesota.

172 OFFER HELP FOR THEIR TEENAGERS

Lure in job candidates with benefits that help prospective employees deal with their teenagers. Programs range from advice on communication, depression and stress to help with homework and choosing the right college, according to Business Insurance. Examples:

Denver-based US West Inc. offers parenting kits that target teens, and the Federal Reserve Bank in Chicago has held workshops for parents of teens.

173 CONSIDER THE COMMUTE
For lower-wage earners, a short commute is key to their decision to take a job. Try to match your job offers accordingly.

174 SPRING FOR A GYM
More than half (58 percent) of 1,058 job-seeking managers surveyed said they want their next employer to pay for their health club memberships; 8 percent expect that perk. Flextime came in a close second at 57 percent among those surveyed by outplacement consulting firm Lee Hecht Harrison.

5
Online Recruiting

If you are not recruiting on the Internet yet, you are really behind the times. In fact, 48 percent of corporate recruiters used the Web to post jobs, according to a survey by the Society for Human Resource Management. Among those looking for senior management positions, 62 percent plan to use the Internet in their job search, a Watson Wyatt Worldwide survey found.

Spending by employers on Internet classified ads was expected to reach more than $1.7 billion, according to Forrester Research Inc. The attractions: Cost savings for employers and the instant feedback that online ads afford. Online job sites also help employers reach Internet-savvy prospects. It costs an average $152 per hire with online recruiting, compared with $1,383 through traditional routes such as temporary agencies, says a report by Thomas Weisel Partners in *The Industry Standard: Intelligence for the Internet Economy*.

The best of online recruiting delivers more of the right candidates, lowers hiring costs and brings convenience to an otherwise cumbersome process, according to *The Industry Standard* (*www.thestandard.com*). That explains why online recruiting has now become the second-highest source of new hires at companies like Microsoft, Sun and Unisys–in each case, it lags behind only employee referral programs.

175 Create Compelling Ads

A compelling ad is key to snagging candidates over the Internet. "You want your online ad to stand out on a crowded job board like a beam of bright light," says recruiter Lou Adler, president of POWERHiring.com in Tustin, California Adler's advice:

Tell them what they will be doing.
Focus at least half your Internet ad on what the person would do on the job and what she would be expected to accomplish.

Tell them what their future could hold.
Paint a picture of how the person can grow and develop on the job. Give them something to reach for and you will attract some of the best people.

Limit the requirements.
Edit your list of required academic credentials and skills down to one sentence. These lists are a big turnoff and exclude the best from even applying.

Use outrageous titles.
Interesting and exciting job titles will make your Internet ad stand out. Get creative. For example, say UNIX Guru not UNIX Administrator Instead of Inside Sales Person, advertise for a Tele-Sales Wizard.

176 Anchor Recruiting to Your Website

Cyber-recruiters are finding it more effective to post openings on their own corporate Websites than on third-party career hubs, a survey shows. Companies that posted jobs for more than 6 months and those that posted more than 50 jobs to date made hires at a faster clip than did less aggressive firms, according to Austin Knight Inc.,/TMP Worldwide, a Sausalito, California recruitment and communications firm.

Among college graduates, 94 percent use corporate Websites in their job search and a quarter of them have rejected employers based solely on their site, according to a survey by WetFeet.com. Survey respondents say they are looking for a clear business description, office locations and specifics about job positions, plus easy navigation on the site and quick download time.

The Hiring Network: 444 Rules to Live By

177 Follow the Leaders
To help you design a recruitment-friendly Website, take a look at these 10 sites considered to have top-notch employee recruiting sections: www.goldmansachs.com; www.bcg.com; www.mckinsey.com; www.bain.com; www.pwc.com; www.ml.com www.microsoft.com; www.morganstanley.com; www.ibm.com; and www.jpmorgan.com.

178 Keep It Simple
Three of every four online job seekers give up in frustration before submitting an application, according to a study of corporate recruiting sites. The main problems: overly complex Websites requiring too many mouse clicks, poor search functions, too many graphics slowing things down and a failure to see things the way an applicant does.

Bottom line: Make sure your job section is easy, says New York-based Web researcher and consultant Mark Hurst, co-author of *E-Recruiting: Online Strategies in the War for Talent*. Hurst estimates that companies with user-friendly recruiting Websites save up to $8,000 in person-hours for each position filled.

179 Present a Dynamic Home Page
Your home page is the first impression you will make on online job prospects. Hit them with up-to-date graphics, your corporate slogan and a powerful message.

180 Keep It Fresh
Nothing turns off job seekers faster than finding out-of-date information on a company's Website. No matter the size of your company, put someone in charge of updating your site.

181 Include FAQs
That acronym so ubiquitous on the Web–standing for frequently asked questions–is particularly useful to job seekers. Ask and answer common questions that prospects might have, such as: What jobs are open? How do I apply? and What is your interviewing process? Customize the FAQs to your company.

182 Use Descriptive Job Titles
When writing your ads, use descriptive job titles that will stand out in a keyword search. Example: Instead of programmer, say visual basic programmer.

183 Do Not Forget the Basics
Make sure your employment site hits the basics: Company history and mission statement, products, HR contacts, office locations and descriptions of the work environment.

184 List Every Job Internally
Micron Electronics Inc. lists almost every job available in the company on an intranet Web page, according to *Human Resources Executive*. When employees find something they like, they click to a page that asks questions and in the process, create a résumé. Their application goes to the hiring manager as well as to a database that managers use when trying to fill jobs.

185 Lure Candidates with Video Clips
HR professionals find that the most effective corporate recruiting Websites offer an intimate look at the company and its staff through company tours, video clips and employee vignettes, according to *Recruiting Trends*.

Example: Microsoft Corp.'s site offers employee profiles and a glimpse into company culture. Even more creative is Cisco Systems Inc.'s Make a Friend@ Cisco program, which encourages job seekers to exchange their résumé for a call from a company employee.

186 Tack on Career Advice
Along with the employment opportunities listed on your company Website, consider adding specific career tips and answers to common job-related questions. Potential candidates will find it easier to approach your firm and deliver a higher-quality application package your way.

187 Make It a Game
Looking for a unique way to attract young applicants while testing their abilities at the same time? Consider an online computer game that tests corporate skills.

The Website of Ernst & Young LLP (*www.ey.com*) allows potential job candidates to become the CEO of a fictional medical equipment manufacturing firm. Growth has stalled and the assignment is to direct a turnaround. Before playing, job seekers input their education and work history. Ernst & Young grades the applicants' efforts on business practices and strategies—and nets a higher level of recruits in the process.

188 Add Links to Your City
Create a link to Websites about your city on your recruiting site. Look for sites from your chamber of commerce, local school districts, sports teams and cultural activities. Getting out-of-town job prospects excited about your location is key to getting them pumped about your job openings.

189 Start Young
Include a page on your Website geared to high school students. Focus on possible career paths and exciting opportunities with your company. Jobshadow.org is a job-shadowing Website that lets high school students learn about a variety of careers. Students can communicate with chefs, computer programmers, scientists and chief executives via the Internet.

190 Link to College Sites
Obtain permission to link your firm's site to those of college and university career centers. That way, future grads can plug into your company effortlessly.

191 Go Global
Nearly 100 percent of the Global 500 will recruit on their corporate Websites to some extent, says the third annual Fortune Global 500 Website Recruiting Survey, by iLogos Research, a division of recruitsoft.com (now part of Taleo).

195 Turn the Tables

Boston-based ReplyTo.com earned the distinction of being the first recruitment Website to pay successful job seekers a hiring bonus for posting their résumé and finding a new position. Money normally spent on recruitment ads by employers is redirected to the job seeker. For employers, this new approach means they pay for an individual job listing only if they locate, hire and retain an employee.

196 Create Profiles for Open Jobs

ResumeAgent, an Internet service for employers and recruiters from Atlanta-based JobBankUSA.com, lets companies create an unlimited number of profiles for open positions. ResumeAgent then queries JobBankUSA.com's master database every 24 hours. Candidate résumés that match the profile are emailed to the employer each day. No fees are assessed after a certain number of uses. Visit *www.jobbankusa.com*.

197 Compare Salary Data

Use the Salary Wizard to find the prevailing compensation rate for particular positions and industries online. Choose an industry and position from a series of drop-down menus, fill in the appropriate job information and ZIP code and get back a detailed salary report for the position in a given locale.

The Salary Wizard, from salary.com, is available on these career Websites: CareerCreations.com; Jobs.com; Vault.com; WetFeet.com; Yahoo!; CollegeRecruiter.com; and Postnet.com.

198 Broaden Keywords

More and more job seekers on the Web are looking for a broader range of interests and job titles. That means your firm should broaden keywords when posting its openings.

"The pool of job seekers using the Internet to find employment continues to expand in all professional areas, including customer service, secretarial and, not surprisingly, entry-level positions," says Bernard S. Hodes, former president of CareerMosaic, one of the largest employment databases (now a part of CareerBuilder.com). By far the most popular searches are for manager/management, followed by sales, engineer, accounting and marketing, in that order. But included in the top 25 are nurse, teacher, customer service and entry level positions.

199 Pay Up for Bells and Whistles

Just posting a job on an employment site might not do the trick. "Use banners, links and upgrades to get prospects off the general job board and onto your posting," says Suzanne Davidson in *Hireadigm: Recruiting News for Professionals*. "Upgraded jobs that appear on the top of employment site search pages are well worth the investment," she says. On CareerBuilder.com, for example, you can pay to appear on the first page of a particular search category.

200 Tie into Local Online Guides

Vault.com and Ticketmaster Online-CitySearch Inc. have partnered to provide job seekers with local jobs and career content via CitySearch's network of online guides for local communities. The attraction for employers: It makes it easier to target local candidates.

CareerBuilder's career center is featured on all the CitySearch.com sites. In turn, CitySearch.com has been added to the CareerBuilder Network, where the company provides private-labeled career centers for nearly 30 major media companies that offer employment classifieds and career-related content.

201 Cast a Wider Net Online

Here is a no-cost way to post job openings online: Tap into America's Job Bank, sponsored by the U.S. Department of Labor and the state-operated Public Employment Service. Because the program is funded through unemployment taxes, there is no charge to employers or job seekers to list jobs or post résumés for 30 days. Visit www.ajb.dni.us to check out more than 50,000 potential new hires.

An improved version of America's Job Bank includes a county search; shopping cart; address book and contact manager; user personal links;

benefits information; express résumé; open résumé format; simplified job/résumé posting; employer profile/company description; and enhanced search engines. The site, which posts more than 300,000 résumés online, is at *www.ajb.dni.us*.

202 LINK UP WITH STATE GOVERNMENTS

Try hooking up with your state government to bring recruits to your state. In Arkansas, a state-developed online recruitment site, *www.ajb.org/ar*, features job listings from Arkansas companies and government agencies. Any company, government agency or nonprofit organization may list its Arkansas job openings on the site at no cost. The listings are continually updated.

For more information, plus clues on how to spur your local economic development authority to explore online recruitment, contact the Arkansas Department of Economic Development, 501.682.5154.

203 CHECK OUT ASSOCIATION SITES

Nine in 10 American adults belong to an association—and four out of 10 belong to at least four of them. That is why targeting your searches to association lists would seem to be a natural. Fortunately, there are free ways to find the associations that would be good matches for your firm:

- Internet Public Library's Associations on the Net, *www.ipl.org/ref/AON*, is a well-categorized collection of more than 1,100 Internet sites that provide information about professional and trade associations, cultural organizations and political parties, as well as academic societies.

- Gateway to Associations Online, *www.asaenet.org/gateway/onlineassocslist.html*, sponsored by the American Society of Association Executives, lists thousands of associations that can be searched by keyword, location or personal interest.

- Virtual Community of Associations Directory, *www.vcanet.org/vca/assns*, allows you to search by key phrase or partial names to locate associations.

Online Recruiting

204 Post Jobs for Free

Post an unlimited number of job openings and search résumé databases for free with *www.jobs.Prohire.com/default.cfm?*, a feature-rich employment directory. The site's AutoSpots feature alerts an employer in real time when a résumé is submitted that matches the criteria of a specific profile. The site is maintained by Jacksonville, Florida-based Creative System Solutions Inc., publisher of the recruitment tracking software RecruitMAX.

205 Surf the Net

If you are looking for high-tech workers, chances are you will find them on the Internet. That is why a contract recruiter for Sun Microsystems spends most of her time surfing Internet job boards, according to *The Industry Standard: Intelligence for the Internet Economy*.

Because she's recruiting Java architects, she likes to cruise through industry-specific sites such as JustJavaJobs.com, but she also goes to general job boards, such as HotJobs.com and Monster.com. It pays to use a mix of big, general job boards and small, specialist sites that produce consistent results, according to *The Industry Standard*.

206 Make Direct Contact

MRINetwork.com, started by search firm Management Recruiters International, offers job seekers direct contact with and advice from 5,000 recruiters in 900 offices worldwide. The recruiters are organized into virtual villages around candidates of similar skills, and they work with candidates and hiring companies. Attraction for employers: the potential for better and faster matches. Visit *www.MRINetwork.com*.

207 Monitor Chat Rooms

Go to chat rooms that attract people in your profession. Monitor the discussion and jump in to make a plug for your company whenever it is appropriate.

208 Target Ads to Niche Sites

Career.com enables employers to target ads to niche Internet sites. This résumé retrieval software searches public résumé databases as well as third-party private databases and returns résumés based on your hiring criteria. Résumés can be stored and searched in a company's private database or sent via email to preset addresses. Various job posting packages are available.

209 Watch for Multiple Listings

"Look for names that come up multiple times in a top talent database search," suggests hiring expert John Sullivan. "That means they have been independently identified by several different employees as being a top talent in their field," he says in *Electronic Recruiting Exchange*.

210 Make Your Ad Easy to Find

"Make sure the important keyword is in your ad," says hiring guru Lou Adler. For example, if you have written an online ad that says Creative Food Expert instead of dietitian, make sure the word dietitian appears somewhere in the copy so the job board search engine can find it. The job title can be anywhere, since the search engine will look through the entire job posting, not just the title, for matches.

"To be sure your ad is easy to find, give it a test drive yourself," Adler suggests. Look at the job from the prospect's perspective and type in possible keywords or phrases. Does your ad pop up?

211 Adopt Their Lingo

Instead of just searching for the typical words describing a candidate, come up with words that a candidate would use—the industry buzzwords and lingo. For example, if you know that Webmasters are likely to talk about ASP, CGI and PERL, use those terms in your Internet search strings.

Online Recruiting

212 TEST SEVERAL SERVICES

"The bottom line in deciding which online job posting service to use? Measure your results by testing several services," suggests John Sumser of Internet Business Network. "Results can vary by industry and profession and only you can tell where the right intersection is for the results you need" he says.

213 TRY AUCTION-STYLE SERVICES

Monster.com, the online careers Website, offers Monster Talent Market, a marketplace within the site, where independent professionals can market their skills and experience in real time directly to employers. Interested companies worldwide can visit the site, pore over candidate profiles and actively bid on those whose services they need. Profiles can be activated for 1-, 3- or 5-day auctions–during which employers can view them and bid. Visit *www.talentmarket.monster.com*.

214 MEASURE AD PERFORMANCE

Martian Logic, an Australian-based firm, offers an Internet-based product called AdLogic that allows employers of all sizes to select, place, track and measure the performance of their recruitment ads. HR managers can browse through an electronic library of ads to learn where and when particular efforts ran, how well they worked and how many qualified candidates they attracted. Visit *www.martianlogic.com/au/adlogic%20Brochure.pdf* for information.

Adlogic gives you control over content, format and the cost of your recruitment advertising. You can publish your ad across any media–in one easy step.

215 TRACK YOUR POSTINGS

Careerbuilder.com's real-time Job Stats area allows companies to track the performance of their postings more quickly and accurately. The free Resource Search tool helps filter applicants before they even apply. The site has also organized its job seeker search sections into five channels representing the most wanted workers in today's job market: sales and marketing, accounting and finance, information technology, engineering and customer service. Careerbuilder.com lists more than 23 million résumés.

216 Spread the Word

The trick is to spread your company's name and its job listings to as many sites as possible. Tracey Claybrooke, president of Claybrooke and Associates, a recruitment research and training organization, recommends using one of the Top 10 national sites. Then find local sites through such means as the chamber of commerce, typing in jobs and city names, directories such as CareerXroads and online newsletters, she says in *Hireadigm: Recruiting News for Professionals*.

217 Zero in on Top Sites

When you are choosing employment sites to use, Peter Weddle, publisher of WEDDLE's—The Newsletter for Successful Online Recruiting, suggests that you look at three factors: 1) the number of unique users, which shows the total candidate pool; 2) page views, which show how long users are staying at the site; and 3) attention span (page view divided by unique users), which indicates whether users are spending time seriously reviewing site content.

218 Post Ads to 700 Sites Instantly

Post your ads to more than 700 Websites at once through a partnership between POWERHiring.com and RecruitUSA. You can also use their eCruiting Site locator to post your job listings specifically to the sites most suited to your openings. Visit *www.powerhiring.com*.

219 Automate Recruiting

Kenexa's Webhire is an automated corporate recruiting package that locates job candidates on the Internet, qualifies them and contacts them. By searching Websites, newsgroups and online résumé databases, the Web spider screens for qualifications—and even commuting distances. It then emails candidates with a link back to the corporate employment site to view the job posting and sends recruiters a ranked list of its findings. Visit *www.webhire.com*.

220 Capitalize on the Bank

View résumés from a bank of more than 35,000 candidates, under an alliance between CareerMag.com and Infohiway.com. The agreement expands Infohiway's content and provides users the option to add recruitment information to their own customized start page. CareerMagazine, one of the largest online employment services, was one of the first Websites dedicated solely to Internet recruitment services. For more details, visit *www.careermag.com.*

221 Name your Preference

Yahoo! HotJobs sorts and ranks candidates according to your criteria. The site connects you to all the résumés stored at Yahoo! HotJobs. Visit *www.hotjobs.yahoo.com*

222 Pick your Employees' Pet Sites

"Ask your employees which professional sites they like, and then put your recruitment ads there," Tracey Claybrooke suggests in *Hireadigm: Recruiting News for Professionals.* "Chances are, if your employees go there, so will some potential good hires."

223 Find Young Professionals

Young Adult Professional Associates Inc. (YAPA), a worldwide membership and recruiting organization in Syracuse, New York offers an interactive Web service to link companies and recruiters with young professionals and recent graduates seeking to enter or move up in the job market. For employers, the service offers prescreening, résumé matching, career fair representation and overnight selective résumé service.

Companies can also promote their organizations online with a custom-built company profile page and be an online mentor to job-seeking members—as a proactive recruitment tool. Visit *www.yapa.com*, or call 888.USA.YAPA (888.872.9272).

224 Zero in on the Northeast

Restrac Inc. and online recruitment site Jobfind have partnered to offer access to Jobfind's Resume Port online résumé database from Restrac's WebHire Network. Using Restrac's WebHire, HR professionals and recruiters can search through more than 50,000 résumés and retrieve qualified candidates from Jobfind's online pool.

Jobfind's 20,000 job postings and 50,000 résumés are geographically focused on the Northeast. Visit *www.jobfind.com* or *www.restrac.com*.

225 Update Postings Automatically

JobDigger software from Los Altos, California-based Career.com is a job-mining tool that automatically extracts data from job postings on company Websites to update the Career.com site, where positions are advertised. The software is essentially an Internet robot, or spider, that seeks and retrieves posted information on job openings. From this, recruiters learn which pages carry outdated, inconsistent or missing information and are able to pull, improve and replace the job data more quickly.

226 Take Advantage of Résumé Sorting

If you handle a constant stream of hundreds of applications, look into computer software that sorts, keys and evaluates résumés according to criteria you devise.

SmartSearch Online from Advanced Personnel Systems Inc., of Oceanside, California allows you to build a private, protected database to store applicant information. The product also can automatically flag résumés appropriate for open positions. Visit *www.Kenexa.com*.

227 Call on Mom

The daVinci Project, a Syracuse, New York-based consortium of companies facing recruiting challenges, has a few new tricks up its sleeve. On Mother's Day, the consortium asked mothers to email loved ones who had moved away from the area to try to lure engineers and computer professionals back to fill job vacancies.

Online Recruiting

The email message? The people who work at these companies are talented, intelligent people who are able to enjoy full lives without long commutes, drive-by shootings, overcrowded school systems and overpriced housing. Do it for your mother!

The group's Website, *www.davincitimes.org*, logged an average of 500,000 hits, 157,000 job searches and 900 résumés a month.

228 Use Email to Broadcast Openings
Send a broadcast email job posting to lists of associations, newsletter subscribers in your field or contacts you have developed. Put a snappy title in the subject line.

229 Mine for Applicants
Think you cannot find passive job seekers online? Ben Klau, vice president of interactive services for Austin Knight Inc./TMP Worldwide, says "applicant mining via special interest forums and news groups can be especially helpful."

230 Find College Grads Online
NACElink Network is the result of an alliance among the National Assoication of Colleges and Employers, DirectEmployers Association and Symplicity Corporation to form a national recruiting network and suite of Web-based recruiting and career services automation tool serving the needs of colleges, employers and job candidates. To find newly minted college graduates in your field, tap into these college networks:

- National Association of Colleges and Employers' Database of College Members, *www.NACElink.com*
- Showcase of Career Office Home Pages, *www.naceweb.org/info_public/careerservices.htm*
- College Board College Search, *www.cbweb1.collegeboard.org/csearch*
- College Opportunities online, *http://nces.ed/gov/ipeds/cool*

231 Offer Electronic Applications

At many Target and Home Depot stores, computers have replaced paper job applications. Computer kiosks, located near Target checkout lanes, replicate paper documents on screen and are designed to widen the pool of applicants by luring the store's shoppers to apply, Target recently told Knight-Ridder Newspapers. The system also speeds up hiring: As soon as the applicant completes the application, a formatted copy is sent to a manager on duty, and qualified applicants can be interviewed on the spot.

Home Depot says electronic applications allow it to share application information with nearby stores that may have a greater need.

232 Promote Internships

Use InternshipPrograms.com to promote internships to more than 20 million college students worldwide. Launched with more than 1,500 co-op and internship listings from companies of all sizes, the site caters to employers, career center professionals, work force novices, career changers and students. Log on to *www.internshipprograms.com*.

233 Recruit Finance Pros

The National Association of Black Accountants operates an online career center to help companies diversify their work force and recruit qualified finance professionals. NABA's Career Center confidentially links jobs with job seekers and will give your firm exposure to the largest pool of African-American financial services professionals in the nation. Contact: 301.474.NABA or *www.nabainc.org*.

234 Check Out Online Mentoring

If you do not have an in-house mentoring program, provide your employees with a list of ementoring outlets. For example, Women in Technology International, based in Sherman Oaks, California provides access to thousands of women who will act as mentors to Website visitors. Mighty Mentors, a service of Minneapolis-based Mighty Media, lets teachers mentor one another via email after they connect online. NursingNet, an online nursing forum and resource, has mentoring programs for nurses and other allied health care workers, according to *USA Today*.

235 Reach Out to Alumni

Network with corporate and college alumni with Alumni.net, an Internet-based service that allows grads to build personal profiles that can be accessed by employers and recruiters. The concept is simple: Many people who are not actively searching for jobs will use Alumni.net to tap into their alumni networks and even though they are not technically in the job market, they will want to keep tabs on their options—and their market value.

At the heart of the Alumni.net site is JobCity.net. It allows visitors to build résumés and post them for prospective employers to view. Then, through a low-cost, fee-based service called JobFlash, member profiles are sorted to find prospects for you. Visit *www.alumni.net*.

236 Go to a Headhunter

Find sourcing, applicant tracking and background verifications from a Web browser through the online service HeadhuntersDirectory.com. Headhunters, executive recruiters and employment agencies, executive search firms, staffing and personnel agencies are listed here to help you find the perfect career opportunity or candidate. This is a directory of professionals that help people find jobs every day and it is free. Visit *www.headhuntersdirectory.com*.

237 Stage Trial Runs

If a Web job board charges an upfront fee, ask for a free trial to test the results. Some Internet résumé services will give you one free posting so that you can assess who's in their database, evaluate the returns and gauge customer service.

238 Streamline the Process

Ad-Star Services Inc., based in Marina Del Ray, California, has joined with mega-site CareerBuilder.com to launch a new online job-posting service. Employers can create, schedule and pay for their recruitment ads directly on the CareerBuilder.com Website. This service extends Ad-Star's remote ad entry solutions to the Web for online and print publishers.

239 Get on Television
Many municipalities have turned to cable television and the local government channel to advertise job openings. Utilizing public access channels, you can advertise job openings to a pre-defined audience.

240 Specialty Databases
Check out the service from RestaurantRecruit.com called ResumeRadar, a new job board and database product tailored to the restaurant industry. ResumeRadar stores, evaluates and tracks résumés and also features a job board with knockout questions. Employers can customize how the résumés are stored and viewed, allowing them to search by name, position, area, status level and by the score of the knockout questions. Features include customized tracking, evaluation and response system. Call 800.266.6996 or visit: *www.restaurantrecruit.com*

241 Test Skill Levels
It is getting easier to test applicants in entry-level office or highly technical positions. Philadelphia-based Kenexa offers Prove It!, which administers tests using software either on-site or online. In addition to software and technical skills, the package tests for data entry, basic office, payroll and customer-service mind-set skills.

Results are quickly ranked as basic, intermediate and advanced and the software measures the number of correct answers in each category and how long the applicant took to perform the tasks. Visit *www.knowitallinc.com*, or call 800.935.6694.

242 Test for the Basics
Test.com Inc. administers an office proficiency assessment and certification exam over the Internet. Applicants are automatically scored on such skills as basic math, language arts and data entry. Visit *www.test.com*.

243 Customize Screening Tests

Testandtrain.com is a Web-based centralized location for employee and student testing. Employers direct potential hires to the test site, where they use an Internet browser to take customized tests. Testandtrain.com then scores and forwards the results to the employer.

Tests can deliver from one to 1,000 questions, covering computer programming languages, arithmetic reasoning, word knowledge, general science or filing skills. Your own tests can be posted to the site as well. Chief selling point: It saves administrative and staff costs of giving and scoring pre-employment tests. Contact *www.testandtrain.com*.

244 Prescreen Applicants

SmartSearch Online is a Web-based software application for the management of information relating to the staffing process; staffing management, sourcing; tracking; prescreening; and reporting.

Once a search is complete the results (lists of names, corresponding résumés and contact history), ranked according to how closely they match your requirements then are displayed on screen. All search criteria is highlighted contextually within the résumé for rapid screening and evaluation. You can be assured that candidate screening takes place as rapidly as possible after the receipt of the information and more importantly all candidates (both current and historical) are reviewed against current job openings. Visit *www.smartsearchonline.com*

245 Qualify Techie Candidates

Check out Brainbench, pre-employment assessment testing that can be integrated right into your hiring process. Brainbench offers more than 600 different assessments to test skills, knowledge, and personality for job types such as administration, call center, finance, health, IT and more. How it works is you set up an online account. Next you select the pre-employment tests based on candidate requirements. Email your candidate a link that will give them access to the test you created (or they can take the test onsite). Test results are emailed to you immediately following the completion of the test. You can view each candidates test result online anytime from one simple report. Contact *www.brainbench.com*

The Hiring Network: 444 Rules to Live By

246 Look for Legal Eagles
Recruit law firm employees over the Web, with EmplawyerNet for Law Firms, a service from LEXIS-NEXIS and EmplawyerNet. The service includes an electronic recruiter function for law firms to monitor a database of thousands of candidate profiles and résumés. If the information in the profiles meets a firm's specific recruiting criteria, it is electronically forwarded to Los Angeles-based EmplawyerNet's database, which tracks thousands of live job listings.

Companies can place jobs in the database with a low-cost membership and begin building their own database of candidates. For details, visit *www.emplawyernet.com*.

247 Find Hispanic Candidates
LatPro.com is a job board for Hispanics and bilingual professionals. If you are a bilingual (Spanish/English or Portuguese/English) or Latino professional interested in job opportunities and career development, you can join LatPro for free. Employers may search the database for free but there is a charge to access candidate contact information. Employers may also post a position and receive responses from pre-screened candidates. Advertising opportunities are also available. Visit *www.latpro.com*

Saludos.com specializes in joining the Hispanic bilingual professional with companies looking for diversity in the workplace. Job seekers are bilingual professionals with a minimum of a B.S. degree. Posting a résumé is free. With more than one million hits a month, Saludos.com is the #1 ranked Hispanic Employment site.

the Hispanic Alliance for Career Enhancement (HACE) provides linkages, services, programs and access for Hispanic professionals to private and public organizations, thereby strengthening the foundation for the professional and economic advancement of the Hispanic community. Visit *www.hace-usa.org*.

iHispano.com is a career site for Hispanic and bilingual professionals, where job-seekers can search job listings (by keywords, industry, and location), post a résumé and find key career tips and employer information. Free to job seekers–employers may post jobs and search résumés. *www.ihispano.com*.

IMDiversity.com is dedicated to providing career and self-development information to all minorities, specifically African Americans, Asian Americans and Pacific Islanders, Latino/Hispanic Americans, Native Americans and women. Visit *www.imdiversity.com*.

248 REACH BILINGUAL WORKERS

Bilingual Employment Specialists Inc., is an organization of recruiting and HR professionals that uses a global, Internet-based database to help match employers with qualified employees with fluent language skills in more than 35 languages. You can find the group at *www.bilingual-employment.com*.

249 FIND TECH, SALES RECRUITING HELP

Career Engine provides specialized e-recruiting and consulting services to match experienced job applicants with employers through confidential résumé hosting and public job postings online. A plus: The site is backed by a team of professionals who have in-depth knowledge of industries, salaries and skills and are focused solely on recruiting and placement.

Career Engine offers category-specific career services; ITClassifieds, SalesClassifieds; Financialpositions.com; Engineeringclassifieds.com; AccountingClassifies.com; and Black World today Careers (*www.TBWCareers.com*). For details, visit *www.careerengine.com*.

250 CHECK OUT THIS TECHIE DATABASE

The Windows NT Job Center is a free, searchable database of tech professionals with network experience. Employers can search thousands of résumés using skills or job responsibilities as keywords and adding locations as well. Companies can also post job openings. The Internet technology firm Beverly Hills Software runs the operation at *www.bhs.com/jobs2*.

The Hiring Network: 444 Rules to Live By

251 **START-UPS: START HERE**
PeopleConnect is a matchmaking staffing service for start-up companies that need employees but do not have cash and unemployed tech veterans who wanted to work and do not need a paycheck right away. The catch-22: In order to attract funding, they needed a team of experienced sales and finance executives. But since they do not yet have funding, they had no money to hire staff.

Many start-ups are caught at precisely that impasse. The solution is PeopleConnect, a San Francisco-based company that specializes in placing executives and tech professionals who are willing to work without pay until VC funding comes through. PeopleConnect, has carved out a small but unique niche in the recruiting world with what they call their "Employees Without Paychecks" program.

Candidates are initially treated as independent contractors and paid with stock options, with an understanding that they will become salaried employees when the company gets VC funding. Contact PeopleConnect at 415.479.3400 or visit *www.peopleconnectstaffing.com*.

252 **FIND A SPECIALIZED WORKER ANYWHERE IN THE WORLD**
Onrecjobs.com is a niche jobsite for the online recruitment industry. If you run a jobsite and are looking for staff, a company looking for recruitment staff with online recruitment knowledge, a supplier who needs to find an employee with online recruitment experience or perhaps you are looking for an analyst with experience of the online recruitment market this is the place to advertise.

Employees may search for free. There is a small monthly charge to employers posting available positions. Visit *www.onrecjobs.com*.

6
The Art of Interviewing

Interviewing is more art than science. The most effective interviewers plan what they are going to ask, but they are also able to ad-lib during the meeting itself. The key to success is being able to elicit meaningful responses from every candidate.

253 BEGIN WITH A PHONE INTERVIEW
Telephone interviews allow applicants to focus more attention on their responses because they are not worrying about their appearance or gestures. Likewise, phone interviews allow you to focus more on the actual content of applicants' responses because you are not distracted by visual cues, according to a study from Carnegie Mellon University's Graduate School of Industrial Administration.

Yet another reason to use the telephone for interviews: It is cheaper than either face-to-face interviews or videoconferencing. "Many of the things we see [when interviewing] are not related to job performance," said author Susan Straus in *HRNews*. Bottom line: Do not discount the value of observing and assessing a candidate in a personal interview situation. But making a detailed phone interview the first point of contact can provide a better initial, accurate picture of the applicant. You can follow up with a face-to-face meeting and skills testing with the most qualified applicants.

The Art of Interviewing

A Typical Phone Screen Might Include the Following:

- Identify yourself and explain the purpose of your call. State that you have received a résumé and that you would like to schedule an initial telephone discussion.
- Clarify an acceptable time for the telephone discussion. Ask whether the applicant has time to talk now or is another time better.
- Ask the applicant 10 screening questions, including–the candidate's interest in the company and position; compensation; relocation; willingness to travel; and previous experience, among others.
- Determine whether to progress further with the candidate.

254 Rehearse before You Call

Keep in mind that you and your company are also being evaluated by every applicant you call. It is essential to plan what you are going to say on the phone and have a method of recording the interviewee's remarks. From this phone call, you will be able to assess phone etiquette and communication skills. By the person's tone of voice and choice of words, you can also discern how enthusiastic he is about the job opening.

255 Make a Good First Impression

Be scrupulous in your interviewing strategies. Managers who interview well bring a competitive edge to their employers in recruiting. First impressions do count.

256 Cover All the Bases

Make sure you fully brief candidates on the position: their responsibilities, salary range and benefits. Communicate your expectations clearly and decisively. Explain performance review procedures.

257 Move the Process Along

Do not drag out the interviewing process. Set a time frame for interviewing and making a decision and stick to it. If you still have not found any good candidates, start over and set a new time frame for your decision.

258 Keep Candidates Informed
Keep candidates informed of the status of the job search. Get back to candidates when you say you will. If you need an extra week to decide, tell them.

259 Stagger Your Interviewing Time
Stagger your work schedule to create 12-hour to 16-hour availability for recruiting and hiring. Job candidates will appreciate your accommodating their need for before- and after-work interviews, and you will open the door to more serious job applicants.

260 Streamline the Process
AT&T Wireless Services has cut the number of interviews held with each job candidate from three to two. The company now screens candidates by phone and then schedules face-to-face interviews, as reported in Workforce Strategies.

261 Use Interview Guidelines
AT&T Wireless Services wrote an interview guidebook, which all supervisors follow when interviewing and hiring. An interview procedures manual is a good idea, especially if it includes questions you can and cannot ask applicants for legal reasons.

262 Tout Training Programs
Let job candidates know about on-the-job training. Fill in the details: How much training they will get, when and in what form. Candidates are more likely to go with a firm that will invest in them.

263 Ask Four Key Questions
A four-question interview can uncover the best predictors of success on the job: A track record of high energy (work ethic, initiative) and team leadership and some level of comparable past performance, according to POWERHiring.com. Lou Adler suggests asking the following questions to uncover details of the candidate's accomplishments:

Online Recruiting

192 — Set Up a Separate Recruiting Site

Make it easier for job candidates to reach you by branding a separate Web address for your company's job listings and recruiting efforts, such as *www.ABCjobs.com*, suggests *Recruiter's Network*. This will keep job seekers from getting lost trying to find the employment section of your general corporate Website.

Plus, an address like *www.ABCcompany.com/HR/employment/joblistings.htm* is just too long, tough to remember and unwieldy to advertise, says the network, which is the association for Internet recruiting.

Tip:
Instead of registering an additional domain name, ask if your IT department or Web-hosting provider can point the shorter address at the existing employment section within your company's Website. For example, when a job seeker types *www.ABCjobs.com*, he is really being linked around your existing domain to *www.planetrecruit.com/index.cgi*–without all that extra typing.

193 — Target Your Ad to the Audience

"Instead of thinking of the job you are trying to fill, think of the kind of person you are seeking," says John Sumser, CEO of Mill Valley, California-based Internet Business Network and editor of *Electronic Recruiting News*.

Say you need a savvy Web developer. You know there is a talented group of pros who work for a Web development company in a Colorado resort town. The employees there like what they do, but they also love snowboarding. Bingo! Target that interest by advertising on a snowboard-enthusiast site, rather than on a giant job board, where your posting may get lost in the crowd.

194 — Tout Your Company's Size

When recruiting online, use your company's size to best advantage. Hot growth opportunity, pre-IPO, fast growing and small firm, big clients are key buzz phrases for today's Internet ads, according to an MSNBC item. Use them–but only if they are true.

The Art of Interviewing

- What has been your most significant accomplishment in each of your past two or three jobs?
- For each of your past two or three jobs, I would like you to sketch out an organizational chart. Can you tell me about your most significant team or management achievement in those positions?
- One of our key objectives for the person who is offered this position will be to _____ [describe a top performance objective]. Can you tell me about your most important comparable accomplishment?
- If you were offered this position, how would you go about implementing _____? [Describe top two or three performance objectives your organization has established for the position.]

264 THEN ASK ONE MORE

If you are feeling good about this candidate, Adler says, ask a fifth question: Although we are meeting with some other fine candidates, I believe you have a strong background. We'd like to get back to you in a few days. What are your thoughts now about this position?

This question shows that you are interested and elicits input on your candidate's level of interest. "You will find this question reveals issues and ideas you will explore during your next interview with the candidate–the interview that will happen just before you make a job offer," Adler says.

265 ASK FOR A BUSINESS CARD

This technique is often overlooked, but it will help you verify the applicant's actual title and employer. By showing you her business card, an applicant establishes more credibility with you.

266 ASK TO RECHECK THE APPLICATION

Once an applicant has filled out a job application, give it back and ask him to check it for any errors or blanks. This demonstrates the importance that your company places on accuracy and honesty–and may make the applicant think twice about lying on the form.

Misstating Qualifications

Misstating information can be unintentional; for example, listing an incorrect date or job title in a résumé or on an application. It can also be quite intentional, meaning that the applicant will use any means possible to improve his or her chances of gaining employment. Even among those who misrepresent the facts, there can be extremes: From the proverbial white lie (e.g. enhanced salary) to gross misrepresentation (e.g. claiming an advanced degree which was never earned).

Lying on applications and résumés is apparently on the rise. According to a Knight-Ridder-Tribune Business News article, a survey conducted by the Society for Human Resource Management determined that more than 60 percent of human resource professionals found inaccuracies on résumés.

267 Ask for Facts

Get the facts you need by asking questions that elicit answers to when, why, how, impact, result, time and so forth, suggests POWERHiring.com. Get details so the candidates cannot underplay or exaggerate their role. Measure the candidates' trends over time.

268 Be Sure to Get Names

Separate honest Abes from liars. As job candidates tell you stories or give examples of their experience or job behavior, get the names of people who can verify those accounts. Say: You mentioned your boss. What's that person's name? Just by asking for names, you can gauge how quickly and forthrightly they supply the information.

269 Learn from Their Last Appraisal

Add this question to your next interview: "Tell me about your last performance appraisal. In which area were you most disappointed?" suggests Paul Falcone in *96 Great Interview Questions to Ask Before You Hire*.

A good answer to this pressure-cooker question would be one that reveals areas of weakness that are really overstrengths, or virtues driven to an extreme that may require tempering–such as someone with real initiative who tends to charge too far ahead on projects. A bad answer is one that tends to blame others for shortcomings, especially for key job characteristics like reliability.

The Art of Interviewing

270 Focus on Accomplishments
Find out what the candidate has actually done, advises POWERHiring.com. Get examples of the candidate's actual role, time and effort involved. Then verify the information with references.

271 Ask about Relationships
Pose specific questions about how the candidate has dealt with conflict on the job. Get details on how she has motivated people. Ask: Can you give me an example of how you have dealt with burnout on the job? How have you pushed a sales group to produce better results?

272 Watch Out for the I Person
Listen to how your interviewees express themselves. At Southwest Airlines, which is famous for its customer service, a person who says I, I, I in the job interview will not get the job. The airline's ferocious commitment to customer service rests on two musts for all recruits: 1) friendliness and 2) an intense work ethic. The airline does not train people to be nice; rather, it looks to hire nice people. And in Southwest's view, nice people are team players who tolerate extreme stress.

273 Team Up on Phone Screening
As you know, anyone can look good on paper; it is often telephone screening that offers quicker insight. Ask other staff members to screen some on-the-fence candidates with you.

274 Focus on the Future
Focus not only on past performance but on the contribution a candidate could make to your company in the future. Ask: What could you bring to this job? How will our company be better off in 2 years because you work here?

275 Conquer Skepticism
One attitude that often surfaces during job interviews is skepticism on the part of the recruit. "Overcoming this situation with well-researched, thoughtful and immediate answers is crucial to

increasing the chances of landing a qualified prospect," say Gale Heritage and Suzanne Davidson, co-founders of The Breckenridge Group Inc., a recruitment training company. Defuse any defensiveness by openly and thoroughly acknowledging any doubts of the applicant and then present your case.

Let us say you have explained that your company provides advanced technical training, but you sense the prospective hire does not believe it. Here is how to proceed:

- **Offer documented proof.**
  Be ready with a list of employees, their start dates and the courses they have completed.
- **Follow up by restating the benefit.**
  Example: As you can see, our commitment to training will give you marketable new skills that will be valuable to you and us.
- **Follow up again by asking if what you presented satisfies the applicant's concerns.**
  If he still seems doubtful, ask what information he would need to be satisfied—such as more data or the telephone numbers of three employees who have benefited from the training. Then deliver on that promise.

276 PLAY THE GIFT GAME
"Improve employee selection with an interview strategy that treats each applicant like a gift-wrapped present—but with a catch," says Carol Quinn, president and founder of Hire Authority, a Norcross, Georgia-based firm that trains businesses in interviewing and hiring skills. "You have to decide if you want this present before you can see what you have," she said in *The EMA Reporter*.

So try to get as many clues as you can to determine if this package is something you really want. Ask yourself: Is there lots of money inside, or is it just a gag gift? In other words, is it a good hire that can add value and profits to my company, or is it a bad hire that could cost us money?

277 USE PANEL INTERVIEWS
Using a panel to interview job candidates has several advantages—you will save time, learn more about the

The Art of Interviewing

candidates and eliminate emotional biases, according to POWERHiring.com. Ask each panel member to review the candidate's résumé before the interview. Also, tell the candidate ahead of time to expect a panel.

Do not use more than three to four interviewers and use a round table to avoid a firing-line approach. Keep the discussion focused by appointing a leader.

278 Give a Character Questionnaire

Job candidates at Davidson Industries Inc. in Franklin, Indiana, are given a 20-question character interview form to gauge levels of trust, commitment and integrity. New employees are given a set of 49 character qualities and are rated and promoted on how they exhibit them. Employees are recognized for specific traits—such as dependability, patience and flexibility—rather than for achievements. The result? Lower turnover and decreased workers' comp costs at the family-owned manufacturing firm.

Pre-Employment Screening

Pre-employment testing has become increasingly popular among employers, large and small. There are tests that screen for aptitude, skills, mental health and drug use. These and other pre-employment screening methods are often used to keep hiring costs to a minimum. As an employer, however, you do not have an automatic right to require testing of prospective employees. You cannot assume the legality of a particular test.

Pre-employment screen must be based on sound business principles. Generally, that means that you cannot test simply because you want to; you must have a valid job-related reason for doing so.

Source: *Fifty plus on Tips When Hiring & Firing Employees* (Encouragement Press, 2007)

279 Set Up a Tour

Take the candidate on a tour of your offices or plant before the interview, advises POWERHiring.com. If possible, arrange to watch a demonstration. This helps you get into a give-and-take with the candidate and sets the stage for a solid interview.

280 Try Role Playing

To help weed out candidates, try role playing during initial phone screening. That is what Ace Personnel in Overland Park, Kansas does. Supervisors role play as unsatisfied customers and ask candidates to pretend to be a restaurant manager. When the candidate asks, How was everything? The customer complains that service was slow.

Here is how answers are measured: If the candidates automatically refund money, that is not so good. Offering to trade a product or give a coupon for a free meal is better. Best, however, is if the applicants probe further to determine why the service was bad—for example, were the waiters too slow, or was it a kitchen mistake? The more questions they ask, the better.

Note

To make sure candidates get a fair shake, Ace carefully scripts its managers' part of the exchange. Ace has found the telephone screening so efficient that it is able to hire about three-quarters of those who meet the challenge. The message: Consider scripting your own phone interview to assess skills that are essential for the job.

281 Cluster Interviews

By scheduling interviews consecutively, you can make better comparisons. Plus, this is a more effective use of your time. Once you are in the interview mode, you will stay in that mode and not get distracted by other work.

282 Make Applicants Call Back

Tailor your interview call-back system to the job for which you are hiring. For example, PSS World Medical Inc. in Jacksonville, Florida, one of the nation's largest medical supplies distributors, employs a special technique for recruiting its sales force. It is dubbed: Call us because we will not call you. After a structured interview at PSS, a candidate for a sales job is likely to hear nothing at all from the company—even if the interviewer desperately wants to hire the applicant. The reason: It is a test of attitude, of the desire to make the sale.

The Art of Interviewing

Says CEO and founder Patrick Kelly, "We want the kind of candidate who will call us back and say, 'Hey, how about that job? Can I come back for another interview?'" Works every time, Kelly writes in his book, *Faster Company: Building the World's Nuttiest, Turn-on-a-Dime, Home-Grown, Billion-Dollar Business.*

283 DOLE OUT HOMEWORK
Give candidates a job-specific project to work on before the interview. This will allow you to have a working discussion on the project during the meeting. You will get a sense of how the candidate would handle the job—and have a more meaningful interview. Plus, the answers you get will give you a strong basis for comparison among candidates.

284 DO NOT GET PERSONAL
Avoid legal problems by staying away from any personal questions. For example, do not ask about age, marital status, children and child-care arrangements, race, religion, national origin, membership in organizations or personal finances. Make sure your questions are only job-related information to determine if the person is qualified to do the job.

Knowing the Law When Hiring Employees

- Equal Employment Act of 1963. This law prohibits wage discrimination by requiring equal pay for equal work.
- Immigration Reform and Control Act of 1986. This law prohibits discrimination against applicants on the basis of national origin or citizenship. It further requires employers to establish each employee's identity and eligibility to work.
- Title VII of the Civil Rights Act of 1964. Title VII prohibits discrimination based on race, color, religion, sex or national origin.
- Americans with Disabilities Act of 1990. This law prohibits employment discrimination against qualified individuals with disabilities.

Source: *50 plus one Tips When Hiring and Firing Employees* (Encouragement Press, 2007)

285 TAP INTO NEW MEDIA
International staffing firm Adecco SA has developed ATM-like machines that allow you to interview applicants in job-shop kiosks at malls and colleges. Applicants are interviewed by touching on-screen answers to questions about education and skills. Adecco then calls promising applicants to arrange personal interviews and employers pay a fee to hire the workers.

286 QUERY MANAGERS ABOUT THEIR HIRES
If you are hiring a manager, ask: Who are the top three people you have recruited? The best candidates will share their success stories and brag about where their star hires are today. If you get a blank stare, do not expect that applicant to assemble a winning team.

287 ASK ABOUT EARLY JOBS
The chief of IBM's largest unit says she does not look only for Ivy League degrees on résumés. Instead, she first looks at the number and type of jobs the applicants took on as teenagers. If those entry-level jobs are not mentioned, she will ask about them during the interview. Reason: Early jobs give insight into the applicant's natural instincts, interests and initiative.

288 STICK TO YOUR SCRIPT
Asking all candidates the same questions will keep you on track and allow you to compare candidates more easily. Of course, you will need to follow up on the specifics of each person's answers. But stick to your interview script and ask every candidate the same questions.

289 USE RATINGS FOR CUSTOMER SERVICE REPS
When hiring customer service staff–who have among the highest turnover of any worker classification–develop a rating form to help you pick the applicants who might work out best. For example, when conducting interviews and making final offer decisions, rate each applicant on these areas, with 1 equaling the lowest and 7 the highest:

The Art of Interviewing

- Knowledge, skills, abilities
- Work experience and education
- Ability to understand and respond to questions
- Ability to communicate ideas
- Manner
- Congeniality with co-workers
- People skills with all types of customers
- Prediction of job satisfaction
- Initiative and productivity based on accomplishments and promotions
- Poise and stability
- Dependability, judged from previous job tenure, increasing levels of responsibility and references

290 CREATE CUSTOMER SERVICE QUESTIONS
Rather than using a general interview form, develop specific questions for customer service positions. Address the skills and knowledge required. For example, ask: Tell me about a time when you went beyond the call of duty in serving a customer; or: What does giving superior customer service mean to you?

291 PLAY MIND GAMES
Some high-tech companies, looking for out-of-the-box thinkers, have begun asking job applicants to solve complicated brain-teasers. Some software companies, for example, say this tactic helps them find creative thinkers.

292 WRITE APPRAISALS IMMEDIATELY
Take notes during the interview. Then jot down your impressions immediately after the interview. Include the good and the not-so-good responses.

293 USE THE SOS METHOD
Explore the SOS formula to get job candidates to respond in an organized way. Seek answers to key questions in

threes: situation-options-solution. If interviewees can summarize the facts, present options and choose a viable solution, you will be better able to judge reasoning ability and decision-making skills.

294 **TALK ABOUT REAL-WORK ISSUES**
Discuss problems and related business issues, suggests POWERHiring.com. Accuracy will increase if the interview is more like a problem-solving session than an inquisition.

295 **SURVEY YOUR CANDIDATES**
Companies regularly survey their customers to gauge their level of satisfaction. Why not ask job applicants for their opinion? GE Medical Systems gives a kind of customer-satisfaction survey to candidates after their interview. Questions probe whether they got enough information about the company before the interview and had positive feelings about the day. By trying this, you will let job candidates know their opinions count. You will also get valuable feedback on your recruiting process.

296 **GIVE OUT LITERATURE**
If a candidate has not already seen printed information on your company, make sure you give her a packet at the end of the interview. That should include your company's annual report, newsletters, product brochures and Website news.

If you are recruiting on a college campus, make sure you take along enough material to hand out. Otherwise, someone who walks away empty-handed will think that she is out of the running for the job. Tell the candidate that you would be happy to answer later any questions she might have about the written material.

297 **BE PRECISE**
How you word interview questions is important. Instead of asking, "Why do you want to work for our company? try," "Why are you considering a job change at this time?"or "What aspects of your last job would you like to avoid in your next job?" advises Gary A. Cluff, founder of Cluff & Associates, a human resources, training and recruitment consulting firm in Reston, Virginia.

The Art of Interviewing

Instead of asking, "How did you get along with your last supervisor?" Cluff suggests: "Tell me about a time when you did not agree with her. How did you handle it?"

298 PROBE FOR ANALYTICAL ABILITY
Do not ask, How do you solve problems? Cluff says. Instead, try saying: Tell me about a particularly difficult job-related problem you faced recently. How did you handle it? What were the results? or Think of a time when you had to gather a lot of data. Talk me through the steps you followed. And what were the results?

299 EVALUATE STRESS TOLERANCE
Instead of asking, Under what conditions do you do your best work? Cluff says you should try this: Think of a time when you were under a lot of pressure at work. What were the circumstances? What did you do? And how did it turn out?

300 ASK YOURSELF ONE QUESTION
The Atlanta-based fast food chain Chick-fil-A rates its store manager candidates highest for character, drive and people skills, according to authors Jim Harris and Joan Brannick. Sometimes these traits count even more than previous restaurant experience. The company has recruiters ask themselves one key question: Would I like to have my son or daughter working for this person?

301 DETERMINE THEIR DREAM JOB
Ask hot prospects to fill out a questionnaire about their dream job, suggests hiring expert John Sullivan in *Electronic Recruiting Exchange*. What are their criteria for accepting a new job? What frustrates them about their current job? What have they always wanted to be?

302 MAKE THE FINAL CUT WITH A TOUR
You have narrowed the field to three job candidates. To choose the best one, give each a tour of your facility. Watch closely how they meet and greet. If they chat freely with executives but

are less enthused with the mailroom clerk, that is a red flag. If they profess complete understanding of the operation and do not ask questions, raise your guard.

303 Ask Rehires about Change

When you are interviewing former employees who want to come back, consider this advice from Virginia Champney, HR manager at Suss Microtech America in Waterbury Center, Vermont, told *HR Magazine*. Ask them this crucial question during your interview: How have you changed so that our company is good for you?

304 Use Silence to Your Advantage

Try this technique if you cannot seem to get an applicant to open up: Do not say anything. Most people cannot bear the quiet and will rush to fill in that dead air time. If you keep silent, the applicant may reveal much more than she had intended.

305 Videotape Finalists

If you have five final candidates for a key post and do not want to spring for five airfare tickets and hotels, interview them via video camera. Many college campuses and outplacement firms already have the technology at their end; you can match it by buying or renting equipment.

If this helps you cut your list of candidates down from five to two, it may be money well spent.

306 Give Applicants a Video Preview

After exit interviews revealed that many employees were leaving because their jobs were so different from what they had expected, Eckerd Corp. produced a 6-minute video to show applicants what working in a drugstore is really like, according to *Workforce Strategies*.

Each candidate for an hourly associate job watches the tape before being interviewed. Described by the company's HR staffing and systems manager as MTV style, the video features employees who tell it like it is and demonstrate the reality of job duties—operating cash registers, stocking shelves, answering customer questions and even cleaning bathrooms.

Managerial applicants see a longer version that describes career advancement opportunities. The payoff: Showing the tape has reduced turnover and produced more informative interviews. Applicants are asking more detailed questions and new hires are better informed about their responsibilities.

307 Prepare Some FAQs

Just as many Websites include frequently asked questions (FAQs), you could prepare a similar list to give to job candidates and new hires. Using a written question and answer (Q&A) format, describe company policies, missions, benefits and culture to introduce your firm in a positive and professional light.

7
Keep New Recruits on the Job

Keeping top recruits on the job is more important than ever before. Studies show that top candidates are not afraid to jump ship early on if they are not satisfied with their new company. Your efforts are well worth it in this area—the cost of replacing a recent hire is staggering.

308 Provide New-Hire Orientation

It pays to think about how new employees come into your company. Oregon-based Sequent Computer Systems (a subsidiary of IBM) assigned a sponsor to all new employees before they began work. The sponsor introduced the new employee to others, rounded up office supplies, showed him how to use the company computer network and email system and gave a general orientation about company culture.

Sponsors volunteered for the orientation duty and committed about 30 minutes a day to their new colleague over the first couple of weeks. The results showed that the benefits to the company far exceed the loss of the half-hour a day of the seasoned employee. The company logged a better new-employee retention rate and considers the sponsor plan an important teamwork builder. Having a peer as sponsor also helped increase the comfort level of the new hire.

Keep New Recruits on the Job

If a company has what it takes to keep its existing employees satisfied and productive, it similarly has what it takes to bring in new talent. The reason people stay at your organization is the same reason they join.
— *Keith Swenson*, former principal, William M. Mercer Inc..

309 SET THEM ON A CAREER PATH
People will stay at your company if they see a future for themselves there. During both formal performance reviews and informal chats, go over possible career paths with them. Then provide the guidance, training and direction to help turn those discussions into reality.

310 KEEP THE JOB INTERESTING
Banish boring routines and rotate employees through a range of projects so they are exposed to many challenges. One of the most motivating aspects of any job is when people can honestly say, Every day is different. Also, give them the autonomy to experiment and function at least somewhat independently. Micromanaging deadens people's desire to go the extra mile.

311 PERSONALIZE JOBS FROM THE GET-GO
At Agilent Technologies in Santa Clara, California, managers are taught to make dreams happen. On their first day of work, new hires are asked these questions:

- What frustrates you?
- What motivates you?
- What do you want to learn?
- Where would you like to be 6 months from now?
- Why did you quit your last job?

This employee-driven approach seems to work: Agilent's turnover rate remains in the single digits, despite cutthroat competition from tech leaders.

312 Collaborate with Your Staff

Treat your staffers as in-house experts. After all, that is what you want them to be. Ask them for advice—you will be letting them know their opinions count, and they will feel like part of the team.

313 Finance Home Computers

This is a win-win for many companies. Finance home computers and you will give new employees a much-welcomed perk and help them hone their computer skills at the same time.

Federal Mogul (formerly Fel-Pro Inc.,) an Illinois-based company, gave an interest-free cash advance of up to $2,250 per full-time employee. The employee repaids the advance within 2 years through payroll deductions.

314 Reward Loyalty with Wheels

At Arcnet, a communications company in Holmdel, New Jersey, employees who stay for at least a year get a new BMW as a reward for their loyalty. The employees get the leased luxury car along with paid car insurance. While the CEO admits the reward is an expensive one, he says it is a lot less expensive than the amount he spent recruiting and training employees during the prior year and a half.

315 Build Loyalty with Short-Term Loans

At Jen-Cyn Enterprises Inc., in Camden, New Jersey, workers who come up short of cash can turn to their employer for help, *Inc.* magazine reports. Jen-Cyn, a galvanized-steel distributor, advanced more than $26,000 to 30 of its 50 workers for financial emergencies.

The loans were used, for example, to put down a security deposit on an apartment or buy a used car. The gesture has a lot to do with the firm's labor pool, in which the median annual household income is about $20,000. Employees repay loans from their wages at $50 to $100 a week.

316 Help with Tuition

With college costs soaring, you will attract and keep employees if you help cover tuition. Nucor Corp. of Charlotte, North Carolina, offered $2,200 a year toward college tuition for up to 4 years for all children of full-time employees. Based on the success of that program, Nucor upped the ante and expanded the benefit to reach all employees, then sweetened the pot even more to cover up to $1,100 a year for 2 years for spouses.

317 Provide Financial Advice

New employees, especially young ones, often need help to get off on the right foot financially. Help them save money on insurance and loans, and steer them toward free financial advice. The online consumer financial network, youdecide.com, does legwork for employees to find the least expensive rates on car, homeowners' and renters' insurance, mortgages, refinancing and home equity loans.

The best news? It does not cost your company a penny. Contact youdecide.com at 770.291.7500 or visit *www.youdecide.com*.

318 Give Them Support

Providing a supportive environment can work wonders toward keeping employees happy in an otherwise stressful environment, such as a law firm. Here is advice from the, director of paralegal and administrative placement at the legal staffing firm Law Resources Inc.:

- Provide opportunities for staff members to get to know one another so they will be more comfortable asking for help when the pressure is on.
- Recognize that people have lives outside work.
- Support them when they must work with a difficult personality.
- Consider instituting a no screaming policy that starts with the firm's partners and filters down.

319 BROADEN WORK ROLES
Even the most brilliant specialist will eventually tire of making the same narrow contribution day in, day out. Use in-house training and interdepartmental teams to broaden employees' understanding of how the company works and how they fit in.

Encourage employees to draw on their full work and life experiences when solving problems or coming up with new ideas. Example: A former retail sales associate now working as a customer service chief may recall a better way to track special orders.

320 ENCOURAGE MENTORING
Employees who have mentors are more likely to stay in their jobs, research shows. In fact, if you do not provide in-house mentoring or career coaching relationships, employees will likely seek them elsewhere–maybe even at a competitor's doorstep.

321 LET KAYAKERS PADDLE RIGHT UP
This will not work for everyone, but if your company is located near the water, consider an idea like this. Seattle-based computer company, WRQ offered free kayak parking to employees. This creative perk is just one reason the firm boasts a low turnover rate of less than 7 percent.

322 REWARD ATTENDANCE, COURTESY
To stem high turnover among school bus drivers, the Midway Independent School District near Waco, Texas, pays bonuses for good performance. Drivers earn $50 per semester for perfect attendance and another $50 per semester for safe driving and good public relations. They get the PR award for not having more than one verified public relations complaint filed against them–such as being disrespectful to students or parents, changing routes without notifying students or not responding appropriately to student problems.

323 Sweeten the Pot for Part-Timers

Offer part-timers the same benefits they received when they worked full-time. The Conference Board finds that most companies it regularly surveys on work force issues have former full-time employees working part-time and 97 percent of the 102 companies offer them some benefits.

Think Time, Not Money

Quality-of-life incentives, such as flexible schedules and training are more effective at keeping new recruits on the job than are cash payoffs, according to a survey of 352 HR executives by the American Management Association. Top retention tools: technical training, employability training and flexible work hours, all of which scored significantly ahead of stock options and pay-for-performance, or bonus, programs.

Among the strategies the surveyed companies used:

Strategy	%
Sending workers to outside conferences and seminars	78%
Reimbursing employees for tuition	67%
Offering managerial training	67%
Supporting employees in degree programs	61%
Offering bonuses	59%
Offering flextime	57%

324 Set Up Vacation Savings Accounts

Everyone knows how important vacations are to one's mental health and continued productivity. But sometimes paying for vacations can just add stress. Some firms set up payroll deduction plans for employees to create personal vacation funds.

325 Join Others to Offer Child Care

A full 43 percent of companies offer some type of child care benefits, a Coopers & Lybrand survey found. If you are a small business, try joining with other small firms to create a cooperative child care center. Or offer child care subsidies and flexible schedules to help ease the child care crunch for your employees.

326 Be Flexible to Stay Competitive

Nearly three-quarters (74 percent) of employers offer flexible work schedules, according to a survey of 1,020 U.S. employers by Hewitt Associates. So if you do not want to be outmaneuvered by your competitors, think about jumping on the trend wagon. The Hewitt survey showed what percentage of employers offered the following options:

Flextime	57%
Part-time work	47%
Job sharing	28%
Telecommuting	28%
Compressed work schedules	20%
Summer hours	12%

327 Think Small

It is not just the high-ticket items that keep employees on board; little things help, too. A Purdue University study of 209 Indiana fast food restaurants found soaring turnover rates but significant improvement when even minor perks were offered.

Those perks included free income tax preparation; interest-free loans for home computers; free car washes; quarterly movie outings; weekly catered lunches; extra vacation for each day the company is profitable; and reimbursed concert tickets.

328 Give Them a Break

Sabbaticals are gaining in popularity because they can improve recruitment and retention. Once the sole province of academia, sabbaticals are being offered in corporate America as a way to recharge employees' batteries and keep them around for the long haul. In one financial services firm, employees get a 3-month, mandatory sabbatical every 7 years with full pay.

329 Compete Head-on with Dot-Coms

Are you competing with Internet companies that are hiring away some of your most productive employees with higher salaries and stock options? Consider what one company plans: It will invest $200 million in ecommerce ventures on behalf of its 14,000 employees and add $200 million to the fund each year. Employees will get a stake in eUnits, whose value will be tied to the performance of the company's AC Ventures arm, with investments in about 20 ebusiness start-ups.

Here is the kicker: The size of the eUnit grants will be based on each employee's tenure and job performance. Under the plan, top-performing managers who have been with the firm at least 3 years could receive as many as 41,000 eUnits. The value of the investment could be several times that when the company liquidates it within 5 years.

330 SPONSOR A WORK/LIFE FAIR
Show your commitment to your employees by bringing work/life resources to them. Using the job fair model, host a fair with vendors representing child care, elder care, resource and referral, health and wellness and community service groups. Try to negotiate discounts for attendees.

331 REACH OUT TO DADS
Make sure the fathers you hire know that work/life benefits are also there for them. "Men who hear about programs for parents usually assume they are only for women," says James Levine, author of *Working Fathers: New Strategies for Balancing Work and Families*.

To reach fathers, make sure company newsletters state specifically that the programs are available to working mothers and fathers. Tell fathers explicitly that your work/life programs are for men, too. Showcase men who have used benefits that others might consider reserved for working women. Print their testimonials in newsletter articles and benefits marketing materials, Levine says.

332 SAVE THEM GROCERY TIME
Employees at the Bay Colony Corporate Center, a technology office park in Waltham, Massachusetts, get a timesaving perk: grocery shopping online from the desktop. Employees tap

into a virtual store and order non-perishable items right from their desks. The groceries can even be delivered to the employer's parking lot or shipped to their home. Employers negotiate a lower monthly fee for employees who sign up or simply offer access to the service at work. Amazon.com and netgrocer.com both offer online grocery shopping.

333 GIVE COMMUTER ADVICE
Get help structuring transportation options for employees, and use commuting benefits to your advantage: to improve recruitment and retention. An employer kit, available from the Association for Commuter Transportation, includes information and strategies for developing and promoting community programs companywide.

The kit explains, documents and updates the most popular kinds of commuting incentives and both the employer and employee tax benefits of using mass transit, car pooling, van pooling or preferred parking. Visit *www.actweb.org* for more information.

334 BE FLEXIBLE ABOUT ADJUSTED HOURS
"Flexible work arrangements that reduce the number of hours a valued employee works can help retain a good employee and also return better performance and productivity for the company," says Shelley MacDermid, director of the Purdue Center for Families. With adjusted schedules, about 90 percent of a group of corporate professionals were happier with how they balanced their work and home lives, MacDermid's research showed.

335 OFFER ONLINE HELP WITH ERRANDS
Cut down on employees' stress by helping them through their day-to-day household to-do list. Circles, a Boston-based firm, offers an in-house, Web-based service with a nationwide team of trained errand runners who will walk a dog, pay bills, book plane tickets, make dinner reservations, pick up dry cleaning, call a taxi and even stand in line at the Department of Motor Vehicles. The service costs an average of $100 a year per employee, according to a *Washington Post* article. Visit *www.circles.com*.

336 Try Transit Vouchers
For new entry- and mid-level employees, the cost of commuting can be a deterrent. Commuter Check Services Corp. offers a transit benefit by which employers buy vouchers for employees, who redeem them for whatever type of pass, ticket, token or fare card they need. The Commuter Checks can be purchased as either a supplemental employee benefit or a tax-free salary deduction. Visit *www.commutercheck.com*.

337 Go with the Pros for Work/Life Advice
Turn to the experts and contract with a consulting firm to answer your employees' work/life questions and concerns. Try Workplace Options, 800.699.8011.

338 Award Stock for Longevity
Silver Diner, a Rockville, Maryland-based chain of eateries, grants shares of common stock to all employees–with a catch. All workers would be granted 100 shares if they were still on the job for 1 full year. In addition, all employees would get an annual profit-sharing stock bonus based on 10 percent of the improvement in operating margin dollars in their restaurant.

339 Hold Managers Responsible
To slow the revolving door, more employers are linking supervisors' pay to turnover, sending managers to retention training and getting midlevel executives to focus on their role in retaining employees.

Example: Hartford Life ties managers' performance reviews and bonuses to recruiting and retention, according to *USA Today*. American Express gives managers a retention tool kit with details on setting up and maintaining mentoring relationships. Retention ability is now evaluated during each Amex manager's review.

340 Help with Elder Care

Offer workers flexible schedules to handle caregiving. Contract with companies that provide elder care resource and referral services. Band together to get discounts with local nonprofit elder care agencies. For ideas and information, contact The Eldercare Locator, 800.677.1116, or log onto www.eldercare.gov, www.caregiving.com or www.elderweb.com.

Few Employees Considered Loyal

Fewer than half of employees feel a strong commitment to their company or believe it deserves their loyalty, according to a study by the Hudson Institute and Walker Information.

The group polled 2,293 employees at firms with 50 or more employees and found one-fourth consider themselves truly loyal and plan to stay at their jobs at least 2 more years. One-third said they would change jobs at the first opportunity while 40 percent described themselves as trapped, meaning they would stay on the job for personal reasons but are not committed to their companies. Half were confident they could find other jobs.

The survey cited six factors that influence employee commitment:

- Being treated and paid fairly.
- The company's care and concern for employees.
- Worker satisfaction with day-to-day activities.
- Employer trust in employees.
- The organization's reputation.
- Work and job resources.

Industries with the highest percentage of loyal employees:

Wholesale trade	31%
Financial services	31%
Insurance	30%
Agriculture/mining/construction	30%

Industries with the biggest percentage of high-risk employees:

Transportation	44%
Business services	42%
Retail trade	41%
Technology	41%

Source: *The Hudson Institute*

341 Offer Language Training

Offering language lessons is a growing practice nationwide, reflecting both a tight labor market and an increasingly international work force. Dallas-based Tuesday Morning Corp. is teaching Spanish to its executives, while employees in its warehouse division learn English. Food manufacturer Major Smith Inc. arranged a series of conversational Spanish lessons for workers and supervisors. And Centex Construction Co. in Fairfax, Virginia, pays for English classes for its workers.

342 Encourage Continuing Education

Send a message to employees that you encourage ongoing education, even if your firm cannot always fund it. Buy and place copies of directories of continuing education scholarships around the workplace. Try: *The Scholarship Book*, published annually by the National Scholarship Research Service and Prentice Hall; *Peterson's Scholarships, Grants and Prizes*, published by Peterson's Guides; and *Peterson's Guide to Distance Learning Programs*.

343 Be a Buddy

San Francisco-based international architectural design firm Gensler pairs each new employee with an experienced professional as a buddy or a mentor, who works closely with the new hire on career goals throughout the person's tenure at the firm.

344 Offer Convenience—at Low Cost

Valassis Communications in Livonia, Michigan, offers such perks as an on-site dry cleaner and hair and nail salon, a caterer on contract to prepare take-home meals, discount coupons for housecleaning services, company cars while employees' cars are in the shop, employee prices negotiated with local retailers and a fitness center. There is more: An on-site doctor 2 days a week, wellness seminars, beepers for expectant parents, 2 weeks' paid leave to new fathers and child care reimbursement.

The conveniences come at no or low cost to the company. For example, the hair salon and caterer simply charge employees who use their services. Still, employees appreciate having them nearby. "They do not have to run around and do so much after work," says a company spokesperson, The result? Easier recruiting and turnover of just 10 percent. "The payoff is in being able to attract really talented people and keep them here."

345 ENLIGHTEN MANAGERS
At the architectural design firm Gensler, managers attend a 3-hour session that focuses on the importance of employee motivation and retention. Plus, employees can attend Gensler University, classes conducted by senior Gensler management and outside consultants. Groups of employees decide for themselves what to study, from company finances to leadership training.

346 HAVE THEIR GRASS MOWED
Busy lawyers do not have time to cut their own grass, the partners at Assigned Council Inc. realized. So the temporary employment service for law firms in Wayne, Pennsylvania, arranges lawn care for attorneys and executives who bring in large accounts.

347 CLEAN THEIR HOMES
Quick Solutions Inc., a computer firm in Columbus, Ohio, sends housekeepers once a month to the homes of employees who have worked there for 3 years. The investment costs the company $60 to $120 a month per employee.

348 CATER TO THEIR PALATES
Employees of some San Francisco Bay area companies do not have to slice, dice, chop or peel their dinner ingredients anymore. Their bosses have arranged for the prepared ingredients to be delivered to their desks. To prepare a gourmet meal at home, the worker just cooks for 15 minutes to 30 minutes according to instructions.

Because their companies have arranged for the service, the employees get 5 percent to 50 percent off the price of the mealkits.

349 PROVIDE FINANCIAL HELP
Help employees get on top of their finances by offering Internet-based financial planning courses via PriceWaterhouseCoopers' Financial Planning Campus. The online tool combines personal finance information with interactive worksheets plus quizzes and audio on topics from cash management to insurance planning. For a demonstration, visit *www.pwc.com*.

8
Target Special Groups

In today's tight job market you cannot ignore the special groups that supply valuable candidates for your expanding work force. Consider seniors: The 55–64 age group will be the fastest-growing segment of the labor force over the next 5 years, according to the Bureau of Labor Statistics. Take a closer look at the nation's largest untapped labor pool: America's 54 million disabled people, where unemployment hovers around 70 percent.

Then there are the teenagers, a prime source of summer help and part-time workers year-round; college students, who will make up your next round of employees; Gen-Xers, a breed of their own who require special care and handling; foreign workers; veterans; and welfare recipients.

Reach each of these groups with efforts targeted at their hot buttons. In this section we will show you how.

350 SUDDENLY SEEKING SENIORS
Senior citizens will be an increasing source of job candidates. Their numbers are swelling by sheer virtue of the nation's demographics–and they now have more economic incentive to work. A new law, signed in April 2000, repealed the Social Security penalty that had applied to working seniors. For years, workers ages 65 to 69 had lost

Social Security benefits to the tune of $1 for every $3 they earned in excess of $17,000. The new law, retroactive to Jan. 1, 2000, means that these older workers no longer will lose any Social Security benefits if they choose to continue working.

There are two important reasons retirees make good hires: They have the work experience and the time. Other pluses: They often are willing to work part-time and they may be willing to forego health benefits if they have coverage through retirement plans or Medicare. But you will have to make some extra effort to attract them.

Who's Who In the Current Work Force

Pre 1946	9 million
Baby boomers (born 1946–62)	61.5 million
Gen-Xers (born 1965–77)	45.0 million
Gen-Yers (born 1978–83)	34.5 million

Source: 2006, RainmakerThinking, Inc.

351 RECRUIT VIA THE INTERNET

Various online tools have sprung up for recruiting older workers. Try these Websites:

- seniorjobbank.org, jobs for the over-50 talent pool runs a nationwide staffing service for older workers.
- seniors4hire.org, jobs for job seekers 50 years of age or older, mature workers, retirees and senior citizens.
- ncoa.org has helpful data and links to other sites.
- fortyplus.org matches older California workers with new jobs. Click on other chapters to find a local Forty Plus group.
- aarp.org, the site of the AARP, formerly the American Association of Retired Persons, is a natural ally in your efforts to hire older workers.

352 PARTICIPATE IN JOB FAIRS FOR SENIORS

Find workers at local job fairs held especially for seniors. The first elderly employment fair in Baltimore County,

Maryland, drew 2,000 seniors to meet with 80 businesses. The Coalition for Older Worker Employment holds an annual job fair and quarterly breakfasts for senior recruitment.

353 TARGET YOUR ADVERTISING
"Advertise job openings in print and electronic outlets that have a large number of older readers, viewers or users," suggests Sheldon Steinhauser, president of Sheldon Steinhauser & Associates, specialists in workplace diversity.

Hardee's restaurants in North Carolina published ads with the headline: Tired of Being Retired, picturing a bored, older man holding a golf bag. Another Hardee's ad, featuring a middle-aged woman about to dive into the pool, reads: How to Ease Back Into the Labor Pool.

354 DO NOT BE SHY
"In addition to identifying your company as an equal opportunity employer, add, This company values workers of all ages," Steinhauser suggests. Use this line in both print and online job ads. In your job promotional materials and on your Website, show pictures of workers of all ages. Use quotes from older workers. Make sure older job prospects see older workers when they come in for interviews.

355 PROPOSE JOB SHARING
Sometimes the pay rate you offer is less important than the fact that the job would interrupt a retiree's long-standing Friday bridge game. And some older workers do not want to work every day, so job sharing between two of them might work well.

356 ADVERTISE IN OTHER SECTIONS
Older people are more likely to be perusing the lifestyle, television or sports section of the paper than the classifieds. So, put your ads in those sections. Or try an ad on your local cable station. Many retirees are not actively looking for a job and do not read traditional employment sections.

Target Special Groups

357 OFFER PHASED RETIREMENT
Are you having trouble attracting older workers? Offer phased retirement approaches, such as reduced work hours and part-time or temporary work. Seventy percent of those surveyed by management consulting firm Watson Wyatt Worldwide of Bethesda, Maryland, said a phased retirement program, along with other flexible work arrangements, is a viable strategy for addressing labor shortages.

358 BRING THEM BACK
Recruit people who have retired from your company for part-time positions—or full-time jobs if they want them. Stress that you need their experience and know-how. But make sure that your retirement policies do not torpedo your efforts if they jeopardize retiree benefits. Check your policies, and change them if necessary.

359 OFFER TEMPING POSITIONS
Retirees who do not want to work even part-time might be willing to be on call. After all, who would make a better temp than someone who worked for you for 20 years?

360 ENTICE THEM WITH COMPUTER TRAINING
Some firms find that it pays to help older workers learn computer skills. Provide training from your resident techies, or pay for outside classes.

361 RECRUIT AT SENIOR EVENTS
Walt Disney Co. recruiters attended the National Senior Games, which drew 12,400 older amateur athletes to Disney World's Wide World of Sports complex in Orlando. The result: More than 5 percent of the participants either took employment materials or completed applications, according to Reuters.

362 CONSIDER RETIREES FROM OTHER FIRMS
Try contacting the HR directors of nearby major companies, especially those that have downsized. They may have a pool of retirees who are eager to work, and they may be eager to help them find work.

363 CHECK OUT FREE HELP

AARP has publications that can help. Up to 25 copies are available free of *How to Recruit Older Workers, How to Manage Older Workers, How to Train Older Workers* and *Valuing Older Workers: A Study in Costs and Productivity*. Order them from AARP Fulfillment, 601 E St. NW, Washington, D.C. 20049. AARP also offers a bimonthly newsletter, *Working Age*, free to employers, managers and decision makers.

364 FIND RETIRED BUSINESS OWNERS

The Service Corps of Retired Executives (SCORE), a unit of the Small Business Administration, maintains a network of nearly 12,000 retired business owners who are available for consulting or part-time work. Call 800.634.0245 for information.

365 ASK TEMP AGENCIES

Temporary staffing agencies often have older workers among their listings. Kelly Services Inc. says. More than 13 percent of its temps are older than 50, according to Research Recommendations.

366 GO WHERE THEY GO

Find out where retirees congregate and target your recruiting efforts. For example, are active seniors in your community going on mall walks to stay physically fit? Get in touch with the organizer and solicit help.

367 REEL IN SENIORS WITH TARGETED BENEFITS

In an effort to boost recruitment of older workers at its company-owned restaurants, McDonald's Corp. offers flexible schedules, management opportunities and for those on Social Security, help with tracking benefits. Currently, about 7 percent, or three workers per restaurant are 60 or older.

Target Special Groups

368 — Tap into Training Programs
CVS Corp., the drugstore chain, is hiring 2,000 workers age 55 and up for entry-level jobs by taking advantage of employment training programs offered through the National Council on the Aging and other nonprofit organizations. The older workers stay on the job almost three times longer than other workers, CVS officials say.

369 — Use a Matching Service
Experience Works is a nationwide matching service for employers and mature workers to fill temporary, temporary-to-permanent or permanent full- and part-time positions. Call 866.EXP.WRKS (866.397.9757).

Recruiting Disabled Workers

It is been more than a decade since Congress passed the Americans with Disabilities Act (ADA), which took full effect in 1994 for anyone employing 15 or more workers. It prohibits discrimination against employees and job candidates with physical, mental or learning disabilities.

Recent studies indicate that Americans with disabilities still face long odds in securing jobs. Only 29 percent of disabled persons of working age (18-64) work full- or part-time, compared to 79 percent of the nondisabled, according to a study by Louis Harris & Associates in cooperation with the National Organization on Disability. And 72 percent of those who are not working would prefer to work.

More employers are starting to reach out to these prospective workers. A report from the Job Accommodation Network (JAN) shows that 27 percent of all cases (2,274 calls) were from employers; 66 percent of those pertained to retaining a current employee with a disability.

370 — Get on the Recruiting List
Employers interested in recruiting qualified people with disabilities can be listed or linked at the Website of the President's Committee on Employment of People with Disabilities. Visit *www.dol.gov/odep*.

371 — Go to the Database
A new database to help businesses recruit and hire people with disabilities has compiled profiles of more than

1,200 job candidates. The free list is available to businesses at their request by writing to the President's Committee on Employment of People with Disabilities, 1331 F St., NW, Washington, D.C. 20004-1107.

The committee, in association with the Department of Defense and the Workforce Recruitment Program, recently sent recruiters to college campuses in 40 states to interview students and recent graduates with disabilities. It plans to update the list with new profiles every spring. Employers requesting the database are free to conduct independent interviews and are under no obligation to hire.

372 Contact the Disability Council
The National Business & Disability Council provides help in finding disabled job candidates, including a résumé database, links to new college graduates who are disabled, an information hotline, training services, newsletter, accessibility services and a library. Contact the council at 201 I.U. Willets Rd., Albertson, New York 11507.

373 Try a Résumé Bank
The National Job Bank is a Website developed specifically for job seekers, employers and employment specialists. Created by executive recruiters and designed to bring those seeking employment and those looking for the best employees available together in one forum. The site is interactive, absolutely free and easy to use. You can search for résumés, post a résumé, post a job listing or contact any of our participants directly. Employers can search résumés by state and category. *www.nationaljobbank.com*.

374 Post Your Job
Post a job for free at *www.worksupport.com* for 30 days. The site also offers resources on the Americans with Disabilities Act, managing disabled employees, creating alternative work arrangements, assistive technology and benefits counseling and work incentives, to name a few.

Target Special Groups

375 GO TO JOB FAIRS

The President's Committee on Employment of People with Disabilities hosts job fairs for the disabled across the country. Visit the Website, *www.dolgov/odep*, for advice, links and information on hiring tax credits.

376 BE SPECIFIC IN YOUR ADS

In your classified or display ads, in the place where you say, Equal Opportunity Employer, add: Women, minorities and people with disabilities encouraged to apply. This will broaden your search tremendously. Plus, you will get points for being a good, community-minded citizen.

377 GET JAN'S ADVICE

For legal advice on complying with the ADA and hiring the disabled, contact the Job Accommodation Network (JAN). The network provides toll-free technical assistance related to workplace accommodations, including one-on-one, cost-effective suggestions for customizing individual situations. Call 800.536.7234.

378 CONSIDER YOUR JOBS

Look over your jobs, with an eye toward people with disabilities. If you have desk jobs available, why not someone in a wheelchair? If your job does not require good verbal skills, a qualified candidate with a speech impediment would be fine.

Earthlink Network Inc., an Internet service provider in Pasadena, California, hired a person who is blind for a technical support position. Speech synthesizer equipment and software helped the employee handle information displayed on the computer and his success on the job encouraged the company to hire four more totally or partially blind workers referred by the Braille Institute of Los Angeles.

379 USE CAUTION IN INTERVIEWS
When interviewing disabled candidates, keep interview questions focused on the applicant's ability to perform specific job duties. Do not ask about disabilities, whether they are apparent or not. Instead of asking candidates whether they can do something, ask how they will do it.

After making a conditional offer, you can ask health-related questions—but only if they relate to the performance of job functions. Before making a final offer, you can discuss what reasonable accommodations may be necessary without placing an undue hardship on your firm.

380 EQUALIZE JOB TESTS
Give the same job-related tests to disabled applicants that you give to others. Be prepared to explain the business necessity of testing. Keep in mind that you may need to provide suitable accommodation for a disabled applicant to take the test.

Scouting for Foreign Workers

It is not nearly as difficult as you may think to hire applicants from foreign countries. A number of new Web-based services can help you with the search.

381 RECRUIT FROM CANADA AND MEXICO
An obscure provision in the North American Free Trade Agreement (NAFTA) allows Canadians and Mexicans to work in the United States legally for up to 1-year under so-called TN visas. Canadians have to pay $56 at the border and fill out forms, while Mexicans have to file an application with the Immigration and Naturalization Service at the embassy or consulate. For details, visit *www.travel.state.gov*.

382 BRING IN WORKERS FOR TRAINING
Small companies are turning to J-1 visas, which allow you to bring in foreign workers for training for up to 18 months. Call the State Department for a list of 120 organizations that can sponsor training.

383 Recruit Foreign Workers for Seasonal Jobs
Do you particularly need seasonal help? Look for foreign workers who are not tied to a U.S. school schedule. That way, they will be able to work through the busy Labor Day weekend and into the fall.

384 Contact Resettlement Agencies
When low unemployment made recruiting difficult, a Baltimore plant contacted a local resettlement agency that finds jobs for refugees. Staff at the resettlement agencies taught the employees key English words, such as the names of tools and then the plant offered on-site English lessons.

"Immigrants make a decision to leave their native country. These are brave, bold people who have decided to seek a better life. If you can tap that, you get hard-working employees," says the HR manager at The American Fireplace Co.

385 Provide Housing
When recruiting from abroad for low-level jobs, the workers' first problem will be where to live. Consider providing dormitory-style housing, as Cedar Point Amusement Park in Sandusky, Ohio, does for its seasonal workers.

386 Look to Puerto Rico
As residents of a U.S. territory, Puerto Ricans do not need visas. That cuts out a whole level of administrative red tape and paperwork.

387 Find a College-Age Match
Check into the New York-based Council on International Educational Exchange, which matches foreign college-age students with companies. For more information visit: *www.ciee.org* or call 212.661.1414.

388 Advertise in Foreign-Language Publications
To reach immigrants and speakers of languages other than English, advertise in the publications they read. Many of these people will be fluent in English as well but like to read newspapers and magazines written in their native language.

389 Have Bilingual Interviewers Available
If you do not speak the native language of the person you are interviewing, find someone in your company who does. Have that person sit in on the interview so the interviewee feels comfortable and to ensure you get all the information you need.

390 Respect Cultural Differences
Let workers choose their holidays. After all, not everyone celebrates the same ones. Decide how many holidays off you will allow, and then draw up a list of holidays, including ones important to people of different nationalities and religions. Then let each employee decide which ones to take off.

391 Appeal to Their Parents
A car wash chain in Albany, New York, recruits in area high schools through guidance counselors and by writing letters to parents and students promising a drug-free workplace with random testing. Some McDonald's stores send letters to parents promising to schedule work hours around schoolwork for students hired before summer begins.

392 Offer Discounts
Recruit teens for summer work by offering discounts on purchases. Extend the discounts for several months after the students return to school to beat your competitors.

Tapping Into Teens

Fortunately, there is always a new crop of teenagers coming up and you will want to be prepared to tap into their talents. While they work part-time and during the summer for you, you can possibly be grooming them for full-time, permanent work later.

How students perceive the workplace

High school students polled by the Families and Work Institute ranked the must haves they need in a career as follows:

Meaningful work	84%
Job security	82%
Work that allows time for personal or family activities	79%
Good benefits, like health insurance	78%
Working with people who treat them well	77%
A job where they can have fun	76%
Being able to earn lots of money	58%
Being able to wear casual clothes to work	27%

As to your needs, the students said they believe employers will demand the following skills the most:

Being able to get the job done, even when tasks are not well defined	75%
Working under pressure and meeting deadlines	74%
Finding creative ways to do their job better or faster	69%
Working with people who come from different racial or ethnic backgrounds	68%
Avoiding and resolving conflicts	67%
Upgrading skills and education	63%

Source: Families and Work Institute

---

393 TRY OUT INTERNSHIPS
Consider offering internship credits or paying for online courses as a way to keep young workers on board when the summer ends. Show your job descriptions to local colleges and universities to get clearance for internship status.

394 Hit 'em Early and Often
Create early name recognition with your future work force. Hold career fairs in high school cafeterias, invite students for office visits or track high-achievers even before they go to college. Meet with guidance and career counselors at local schools and offer to help students explore their career goals through visits to your workplace, mentoring arrangements or internships.

395 Offer a Cool Place to Work
Teens want to have fun. Price Chopper, in Schenectady, New York, ran radio ads on a popular rock station, inviting teens to drop by the store and fill out an application. That qualified them for a turkey bowl where they rolled frozen turkeys down the frozen-food aisle at bowling pins fashioned from soda bottles. The grand prize was a stint as a guest disc jockey on the radio station. The company's objective: To position Price Chopper as a cool place to work and to attract job applicants. It did both.

396 Take Advantage of Free Ads
In a nod to supporting youth and employment advertisers, several major daily newspapers, including *The Washington Post*, are starting to offer free classifieds to advertise summer jobs or internships at certain periods prior to peak hiring season. Check your area newspapers for their policies.

397 Dress Down
When recruiting high school students, dress casually. Teens will feel less intimidated and be more receptive to you.

398 Get on the Web
Teens spend a huge amount of time surfing the Internet. Promote openings that teens could fill on Websites such as www.summerjobs.com and www.coolworks.com.

Target Special Groups

399 TEAM WITH SCHOOLS
Real Life 101 is a 4-year program from the Manatee County, Florida, Chamber of Commerce that teachers 9th-graders about reliability, performance and communication in the workplace through seminars and hands-on work experience in local businesses.

Texas Instruments Inc. lets high school students visit and tour its Dallas offices and company representatives meet with students to discuss education and careers. Fujitsu Network Communications plans internships for high schoolers with mentoring by company engineers.

400 PARTNER WITH STATE GOVERNMENTS
New Hampshire targets high school seniors with its Insights Into Industry, A Future in New Hampshire program, which is aimed at raising awareness about career-track employment opportunities in the state, according to *Employment Security Quarterly*. Employee service representatives from New Hampshire's employment security office accompany HR staff from participating companies to make presentations at schools in their regions.

Information on the job search, application and interview process is provided, along with a regional career guidebook that gives further information about local companies, entry-level positions, skill requirements and wages and benefits. Students also view a video that weaves together interviews with employees who share their job fears and expectations—and then tell in their own words what opportunities exist for their peers. Employers report a higher flow of qualified candidates and better employee/employer matches.

401 GIVE END-OF-SUMMER BONUSES
To keep those summer workers there to the end, pay them a bonus on their last day of the season.

402 CULTIVATE RELATIONS WITH FACULTY AND STAFF
Consider how faculty and staff view your company. Do you have a good relationship? Cultivate relationships among those grooming and steering your future employees.

The Hiring Network: 444 Rules to Live By

403 CHECK RESULTS
Before each college visit, check the results of your last recruiting visit to that college site. Analyze how you did in drawing interviews and how many interviews yielded offers and placements. Use that information in future recruiting visits.

404 HIT THE BEACH
Want to find college students? Go where they go–South. Each spring employers flock to the annual Spring Break Career Expo in Panama City, Florida, South Padre Island, Texas and Lake Havasu, Arizona. The 2000 events draw large crouds of college students in each location. Visit *www.ejobexpo.com*, or call 800.252.4757.

405 MAKE YOURSELF AN EMPLOYER OF CHOICE
CollegeGrad.com is a high-traffic, entry level job site for college students and recent grads. The Website is linked to by more colleges and universities than any other career site and the site is open and accessible by all–there are no passwords or access restrictions on searching job postings, so you can reach all students at all campuses. CollegeGrad has been ranked as the most popular entry level job site by Yahoo and Alexa for providing college students and recent grads with more career information than is available at any other site on the Web.

Employers enter job postings online at CollegeGrad.com to have immediate access to candidates. Companies can also place internship postings at a site for access to undergrads throughout the U.S. and Canada. CollegeGrad also publish the list of Top Employers of the Year. Visit *www.collgegrad.com*.

406 SEND A POSTCARD
Send virtual postcards via a simple email message telling about job opportunities. This tactic works especially well for targeting college students, according to a report on SHRM Online.

407 TAP ON-STAFF GRADUATES
Use employees who graduated from the colleges you plan to visit to carry your message. Nothing cultivates

Target Special Groups

relationships with recruits faster than talking with an alum. Employees who have not been out of school long are the best contacts for your new recruits.

408 GIVE 'EM WHEELS
Many people, especially those who lived on campus, graduate from college without a car. Offer to rent them a car for several months until they can save up for a down payment on one of their own.

409 PROMOTE ADVANCEMENT OPPORTUNITIES
Spell out clearly the opportunities for advancement at your firm. A national poll of college students, conducted by Students in Free Enterprise of Springfield, Missouri, found that opportunity for advancement is the No. 1 attribute they look for in an employer.

410 PROVIDE ONLINE CAREER GUIDANCE
In what may prove to be an emerging trend, Dallas-based Texas Instruments Inc. offers a career planning service on its Website for use by graduating college seniors. The free service lets students test their ability to do certain jobs, match skills and interest with opportunities and learn how to handle interview and job offers. The site includes advice on résumé preparation, a schedule of campus recruitment visits and a career mapper to help students with job searches, according to *The Wall Street Journal Interactive Edition*.

"We have found that students who use the Website are better candidates for jobs at TI because they are more prepared and because TI is able to better match the right skills and talent with the best job candidate and position," says the recruiting director at a staffing agency.

411 DO AN IN-HOUSE REVIEW
Ask employees—especially your more recent college grads—to review your campus recruiting materials. Listen to their suggestions for improvements.

412 Provide Temporary Housing

New college grads will need a place to live. Provide an apartment or a room in an extended-stay hotel for a few months to give them time to find a suitable place to live.

413 Grow Your Own

If you cannot find the college grads you need, partner with a college to design your own program. That is what the Walt Disney Co. did. The company that Mickey built has partnered with California State–Fullerton to create a multidisciplinary concentration in entertainment and tourism. The six-course curriculum will be aimed at arts, business administration and communications majors. A company official said Disney hopes the program will become an industry feeder.

Top-Rated College Recruiting Methods

On-campus recruiting still ranks as the No. 1 way to find college applicants. Here is how other methods fared on a 5-point scale, with 1 = Not at All Effective and 5 = Extremely Effective.

On-campus recruiting	4.30
Company's co-op program	3.90
Company's internship program	3.82
Career/job fairs	3.74
Employee referrals	3.72
Faculty contacts	3.41
Student organizations/clubs	3.38
Internet job postings (own Website)	3.34
Internet postings (commercial site)	3.27
Requesting résumés from career offices	3.23

Source: National Association of Colleges and Employers

414 Make a Direct Appeal—with Pizza

Instead of giving away T-shirts, hats and mouse pads emblazoned with the company logo, Cisco appeals directly to students. The Internet networking firm sends pizzas to university residence halls when students are studying for final exams, according to *Finding &*

Target Special Groups

Keeping Great Employees by Jim Harris and Joan Brannick. A note on the pizza box wishes them good luck as they wrap up their studies—and reminds them to visit the Cisco Website, just in case you would like to apply.

415 Lure Students with Lucrative Internships

Become more creative in selling your image to college graduates. Take the example of Louisville, Kentucky, where Bulldogs in the Bluegrass brings students from Yale University in New Haven, Connecticut, to Louisville for summer internships with a guaranteed salary of $3,000 a month and free lodging in dorms. The result? Five of 35 interns in the first Bluegrass program returned to the city for permanent jobs, Mike Bosc, vice president of communications for the Greater Louisville Inc. Metro Chamber of Commerce, told the *Lexington Herald-Leader*.

416 Get Tabletop Ads

Reach college students where they hang out—in cafeterias, food courts, student unions and cybercafes. How? A new concept in recruiting puts your company's message right under their noses—on the tables where they eat, talk and gather. College tabletop advertising is the brainchild of Benning & Associates, based in Mystic, Connecticut.

Through custom-designed dining tabletops, employers' full-color recruitment ads are placed in the most heavily used common areas. An internship, co-op or recruitment ad can appear for 1-year at one or all participating schools, and you can update or change the ad every 8 weeks. Prices vary by the number of tables and schools and are usually for a one- or two-table buy at one college running a year. Companies report an increase in job-fair and open-house traffic and more knowledgeable applicants because of the tabletop marketing. Contact Creatable Media, Inc., Woodland Hills, California, 818.884.7141 or visit: *www.creatablemedia.com*.

417 Be Quick with Job Offers

Decide which college interns will get your job offers, and tender your offer by the end of the summer. Give them a deadline for responding, but include a clause that gives you the option to match any offer they receive during the school year.

418 Be an Early Bird

To get the pick of the litter, schedule your college recruiting visits as early in the academic year as possible. Be at the first on-campus job fairs and make follow-up visits throughout the year.

419 Offer a Job—Even if You Do Not Have One

Framingham, Massachusetts-based Staples Inc., takes what it calls a job-or-no-job approach to hiring promising new MBAs. The office supply chain brings several of them on board without having specific job openings for them.

The retailer lets the grads work for the first few months as professional floaters doing different jobs in many departments until they become familiar with company operations. The tactic has two main benefits, Staples reports. First, the new hires gain hands-on experience in a variety of jobs. Second, the company gets a chance to observe them in various situations, get feedback from managers and co-workers and then use this information to make a permanent placement decision.

420 Go Online for Interns

Technology-savvy students are turning away from traditional job-search methods in favor of online sources. Follow their lead by advertising online for interns or seasonal help. Try these sites: www.summerjobs.com; www.coolworks.com; www.internshipprograms.com; www.jobweb.com and www.studentsearch.com.

421 Offer a Lottery

Sun Microsystems tries to entice next-generation employees during road recruitment trips with the chance to win new Ultra 5 workstations loaded with software. Some 1,500 people registered for the company's first stop at the University of Washington in Seattle. The company planned to hit Boston and then several Asian stops, according to *Tech Web*.

Target Special Groups

422 TAKE ADVANTAGE OF SPRING BREAK
Externships for college students are catching on fast. Externs toil for free during shorter periods, usually during semester breaks or in the spring. The students get a foot in the door, and employers get a chance to evaluate them for internships, as well as future hires. Call the business school at your local college or university to see if they offer extern programs.

423 MAKE A DIGITAL SPLASH
Advertise in the Digital Guidebook Series, a high-tech approach to college guides. The series, in CD-ROM format, is distributed to career centers at 4-year colleges and universities. The digital approach offers a multimedia presentation for employers and gives job candidates immediate access to company Websites. For a free information kit from Hobsons Corporate Publishing, call 800.927.8439.

424 OFFER STOCK OPTIONS TO INTERNS
The days of unpaid internships may be gone for good now that interns know their worth in this tight labor market, suggests *Wired News*. Take the lead from technology firms by offering interns stock options as payment. The idea just might take off after two Massachusetts Institute of Technology students became millionaires from stock options acquired during a brief internship at a start-up firm.

425 DO NOT OVERLOOK LIBERAL ARTS GRADS
These kids often have a mix of skills that will make them good job applicants. If you cannot find enough technical grads to fill all your slots, hire some bright liberal arts students and train them.

426 INTERVIEW SCREENED CANDIDATES
Find prescreened students who are at the top of their class with help from Collegerecruiter.com which helps companies and organizations find qualified interns. Wetfeet.com and InternWeb.com are also good sources.

Going After Gen-Xers

There are not too many of them, and you need to tailor your recruitment and on-the-job efforts to their style. Be warned: casual days are not enough. These young, sought-after employees can be a tad more demanding than that. Here are some tips for recruiting Gen-Xers.

427 Do Not Fake It
If you want to hire younger people, tell it like it is, say recruiters who specialize in this area. Gen-Xers loathe hype. Appeal to their goals by citing examples of successful employees in the same age group in your company.

428 Do Not Sugarcoat Life on the Job
If everyone has to answer the phone and open the mail, say so. Gen-Xers want to know what to expect. Do not try to mislead them with lofty promises.

429 Find Out What Motivates the Applicant
Is it working independently, having the opportunity to attend industry seminars to update skills or creating new product ideas? If these are things you can deliver, saying so will get your relationship off to a fast start.

430 Get to the Point
Gen-Xers want you to be direct. Tighten recruitment copy, perhaps using lists, not paragraphs. Flowery phrases along the lines of–Someday, all this will be yours do not cut it. Gen-Xers want to know:

- What is the job?
- Where do people like them fit in?
- What is in it for them?
- What technological skills can they acquire?
- Will they be able to make a contribution to others?

Target Special Groups

431 GIVE THEM SHORT-TERM PROJECTS
Gen-Xers want to tackle problems directly and move on. They prefer tasks that can be completed in a few weeks or months, not years.

432 OFFER THEM INTERESTING JOBS–AND TECHNOLOGY
Gen-Xers want to work at something exciting and entertaining. They love technology: That translates into PCs, the Internet and anything else electronic.

433 ADAPT YOUR SUPERVISION
Adapt your training and corporate communications to appeal to this portion of the work force. Consider the example of Macy's East: The retailing giant sent top managers to a class on supervising Gen-Xers and motivating retail employees, provided young employees with a road map of career development and described how to succeed at the company, according to an Associated Press story.

Vying for Veterans

You can receive up to $12,000 in federal payments for hiring and training a veteran separated from the military services. If you take on a military trainee, you can receive up to 50 percent of the training costs, not to exceed half the first year's wages. (For details, contact your local employment service office.)

Financial rewards are not the only reason to hire in this group. They are trained, disciplined and adapted to mobility. Here is how to herd them into your company.

434 GO DIRECTLY TO THE SOURCE
Bypass search firms and use no-cost programs sponsored by the federal government to recruit experienced military veterans. The Department of Defense operates two résumé and referral services that allow civilian employers to tap the military labor pool: The Defense Outplacement Referral System and the Transition Bulletin Board. Call the DOD Help Desk at 800.727.3677, or learn about posting jobs at *www.dmdc.osd.mil/ot*.

The Hiring Network: 444 Rules to Live By

435 POST JOBS ONLINE FOR FREE
The Retired Officers Association operates an online job-posting service and résumé database that is free to employers. Visit *www.roa.org/site/pageserver,* or call 800.245.TROA.

436 CHECK OUT A DATABASE
TAOnline.com, one of the very first e-recruiting sites for the hundreds of thousands of job seekers from the military community (active service members, veterans, DoD civilians, spouses, family members and others), has successfully placed military talent in civilian jobs for close to decade. Founded by former military personnel, TAOnline.com has been recognized by industry experts as a leader in providing veteran jobs.

Through an alliance with the Reserve Officers Association (ROA) and other military organizations serve approximately 200,000 service members who transition from active duty every year, there are hundreds of thousands of Veterans, Reservists, Retirees, Guardsmen and working spouses who are looking for new civilian jobs and other career opportunities. These individuals offer the skills, training and experience needed in virtually every industry including IT, telecom, logistics, security and health care. Job seekers are often located near employers, or if not, the military will pay most if not all of the relocation expenses for transitioning service members, making it very economical to hire these individuals. Visit *www.TAOline.com* or call 888.213.8587.

Finding Welfare Recipients

The national Welfare to Work Partnership, at (888) USA.Job1, is not the only game in town. To tap into local efforts to move welfare recipients into the work force, check with your local or state welfare department. Also consider the following tips.

437 CHECK OUT ONE-STOP SHOPPING
Find One-Stop Career Centers that combine training, education and employment programs under the federal Workforce Investment Act of 1998. Services include free or very low-cost recruitment and prescreening of applicants, help with posting job listings on

America's Job Bank, wage and labor-market data and compliance advice on federal laws, according to the executive director of the National Association of Workforce Development Professionals (NAWDP).

Many one-stop services also provide interview rooms, classes in English as a second language and training. For more information, contact your state department of labor or visit the U.S. Department of Labor's Employment and Training Administration Website at *www.ttrc.doleta.gov/onestop*.

438 FORM A PARTNERSHIP

Borg-Warner Security Services in New York worked with Business Link to hire 1,000 former welfare recipients. Standard Furniture, a family-owned company in Bay Minette, Alabama, developed a curriculum with the Faulkner State Community College Adult Education Program to train welfare recipients for specific jobs in its firm. Cleveland-based KeyCorp linked up with Cleveland Works to find employees and then developed its own in-house training, Key Services College.

Go to *www.businessinterfaceinc.com* to find other examples of what employers are doing in this area.

439 SOLVE TRANSPORTATION PROBLEMS

One of the biggest problems for welfare recipients who want to work is transportation. Provide help navigating public transportation systems and offer discounted fare cards. For example, UPS in Philadelphia implemented a bus system to transport workers.

Home Care Associates in Philadelphia badly needed employees at its suburban locations. It had been hiring former welfare recipients, but they often could not afford cars and public transit did not reach some out-of-the-way job sites. The solution: The firm bought small used cars like Geo Metros for the workers. It asked them to agree not to use the cars outside the area during nonbusiness hours. The program costs the company about $80 per week per employee for insurance, maintenance and gas.

440 WORK WITH LOCAL PROGRAMS
Find local programs that screen applicants and locate or develop targeted training programs for welfare recipients. Check with your local chamber of commerce or city hall for details.

441 HIRE INTERNS
Internships are not just for college students. Create an internship program for welfare-to-work candidates. Provide basic instruction and on-the-job training.

442 CHECK OUT TAX SAVINGS
A federal tax credit reduces federal corporate income taxes when a company employs a recipient of Temporary Assistance to Needy Families (TANF) or an employee who had been on welfare at least 18 consecutive months. The Work Opportunity Tax Credit provides a credit for hiring TANF recipients not eligible for the federal Welfare to Work Credit.

443 LOOK INTO STATE PROGRAMS
Some states offer tax credits and others offer wage subsidies for hiring welfare recipients. The worker continues to receive TANF instead of wages during the trial period, and the employer avoids administrative hassles and the expense of hiring until the worker proves himself.

Many welfare-to-work programs offer screening, training and no-interest loans to businesses that hire TANF recipients. Contact your state welfare agency, or visit *www.acf.hhs.gov/programs/ofa*.

444 GO ONLINE FOR ADVICE
The Welfare to Work Partnership offers advice on hiring welfare recipients and information from employers who have been there. Visit *www.welfaretowork.org*. Another resource is the Welfare Information Network, at *www.financeproject.org/irc/win.asp*.

Appendix I
Glossary

A

action plan A detailed solution for a business or hiring problem.

active listening The skill of concentrating on another person or that person's message, which is particularly important when interviewing candidates for employment.

Advertisment These are techniques use to communication vacancies within an organization, including online, on the bulletin board, in newspapers and a variety of ther means.

Affirmative action Refers to programs whose objective is compliance with the equal employment clauses found in civil rights legislations.

Age Discrimination in Employment Act of 1967 This is a federal law which promotes employment for individuals from age 40 to 75. It makes it illegal to discriminate against older workers in all areas of employment.

apprenticeship programs A system that dates back centuries in which a potential craftsperson becomes the assistant of a trained, experienced artisan for a certain length of time to learn the craft or trade.

Americans with Disabilities Act of 1990 (ADA) This act is designed to protect the rights of disabled Americans, it is an extension of the Rehabilitation Act of 1973 in that it pertains to both the private sector and local and state government, regardless of whether they receive any money from the federal government.

area wage survey A survey of what is being paid for particular employment at various levels of experience. Such a survey can be undertaken by individual companies. A more formal survey is published each year by the U.S. Bureau of Labor Statistics.

Assessment center Employers use these centers to observe potential employees at work, often using simulated work tasks to see how they function in a typical work environment.

B

background checking This is a process whereby an employer gathers information about a job applicant from people familiar with that person in past situations-generally, teachers, previous employers and friends. For some kinds of employment, the process can also involve checking credit history and court records.

benefits A generic term covering all compensation that is not strictly wages/salary (e.g., medical and dental insurance, financial assistance, 401(k) plans, and profit sharing). Some benefits are government-mandated Social Security benefits, such as unemployment compensation and workers' compensation. Employers generally agree that they can attract the best employees with attractive benefits packages. Benefits now account for more than one-third of the cost of employee compensation in the United States.

bona fide occupational qualification (BFOQ) Employers may discriminate on the basis of religion, age, national origin, or sex if one or more or those characteristics is a BFOQ for that position. For example, if the job on offer is that of caretaker in a men's locker room, then being male is a BFOQ for that position. Race may never be used as a BFOQ.

business intelligence Not a form of business spying but rather the collection of data from legitimate sources (the companies themselves, professional associations, or the press) about the plans, operations, products, and success of other companies.

business necessity That which must be proven by an employer-defendant when an employee claims discrimination. Employers must show that the company's practices are crucial to the conduct of that company's business.

C

career counseling Helping employees learn more about their own capabilities, limitations, and objectives, including where they stand in an organization, that opportunities are available to them and what they will need in the way of training and experience to take advantage of those opportunities.

career mobility A person's propensity (and ability) to make several career changes in a lifetime rather than committing to a lifelong career in one particular field.

career pathing (CP) Also called career ladder. A series of steps and progressions to achieve a particular career objective in which an individual focuses on three goals: (1) developmental goals; (2) activities necessary to achieve those goals; and (3) appropriate timing.

child care benefit The Family and Medical Leave Act (FMLA) of 1993 mandates that all employers with 50 or more employees must offer as a benefit an unpaid leave of absence for the birth or adoption of an employee's child; some other smaller employers, though not legally obliged to do so, follow suit.

Civil Rights Act of 1964 Title VII This act provides that an individual cannot be denied a job or not be treated fairly on the job because of race, color, religion, national origin or sex.

coaching On-site training used to enhance the abilities and skills of entry-level trainees and managers. A coach (who might be a supervisor but could also be a peer) sets goals that are difficult but can be attained, monitors the employee's attempt to reach those goals, and provides feedback along the way. The advantage of coaching, besides this feedback, is that it enables employees to learn methods to improve their job performance and opens up lines of communication between various members of staff.

comparable worth The idea that pay should be based on an individual's worth (or a job's worth) within a particular organization or society at large. This concept is often employed in considering questions of gender.

Compensation package This is a process of determining the total wages and benefits for an employee or a class of employees.

Contract This is an agreement between an employer and an employee that consists of an offer and acceptance, a competent person, consideration (pay), legal subject matter (nothing illegal in the contract) and proper form.

countercyclical hiring A staffing strategy whereby companies recruit employees, particularly managerial personnel, during economic downturns when more of such people are available. Those who practice countercyclical hiring believe that they are creating a competitive advantage for themselves, as they will be staffed by highly competent people when there is an economic revival.

Criminal background check This process is used by employers to check both references and credentials of potential employees, particularly by search police records for criminal activity.

D

disabled/handicapped workers A category of persons protected under the anti employment-discrimination provisions of the Americans with Disabilities Act of 1990. Disabled persons are defined as those who have a physical or mental impairment that limits at least one major life activity.

diversity In human resources, the concept that any company's workplace should include people of varying backgrounds, reflecting, if possible, the demographics of the area in which the company is located.

E

employee assistance programs (EAP) Any employer-sponsored program designed to help employees with personal programs that are interfering with their performance of their jobs. Such problems could include drug or alcohol abuse; marital or family care problems; or HIV/AIDS or other debilitating diseases.

employment at will The agreement between employer and employee that provides freedom of action-the employee may leave a job at any time and for whatever reason (usually, though, the employee is asked to give appropriate notice); likewise, the employer can terminate the employee at any time and for any reason. Although this agreement is almost universally assumed in any employment arrangement, it is best for both parties if this agreement is put in writing.

employee relations Generally, these are strategies and policies which affect the relationship between the employer and employee, e.g. collective bargaining, communication to employees and so forth.

employment agency This are typically private companies that help clients search for employees and charge either the client or the hiring company.

employment test This can be anyone of a series of pre-employment examinations to test intelligence, aptitude, ability and interest to determine qualifications for employment. A drug test can also be a form of employment test.

Equal Employment Opportunity Commission This agency investigates charges of discrimination and can litigate charges against a company not found in compliance with the law.

Equal Pay Act of 1963 This federal law requires all employers to pay equal wages for equal work, regardless of sex.

The Hiring Network: 444 Rules to Live By

Evaluation Companies use a formal process to understand the strengths and weaknesses of employees, especially if they are new. The evaluation is often the basis for raises and promotions–and sometimes firing an employee.

F

Fair Labor Standards Act (FLSA) of 1938 A law that mandates certain basic requirements of the U.S. workplace having to do with (1) minimum wage; (2) overtime pay; (3) equal pay; (4) record-keeping requirements; and (5) child labor laws. Only certain professional and administrative employees are exempt from FLSA provisions.

Family Medical Leave Act of 1993 This federal law allows workers to take up to 12 weeks of unpaid leave for personal or family health reasons.

G

gender issues in employment compensation The Equal Pay Act and the Civil Rights Act both disallow sex discrimination in paying employees. If a man and woman are both doing similar jobs (unless there is a question of seniority involved), they must be paid comparable wages.

glass ceiling A slang term originally used to describe the phenomenon whereby women would rise to certain positions in companies, as a result of their abilities, then be unable to rise any further, despite their qualifications to do so–a phenomenon that is the result of gender prejudice.

H

human resources administration This is a broad term covering the management of such areas as recruitment, selection, placement, firing, compensation, development, performance evaluation and collective negotiations with employees for a company.

human resources forecasting An effort to estimate the need for workers by using various statistical and analytical methods.

I

independent contractors Self-employed people who work for an individual client or for a company for a specified period of time, usually to complete a particular project. They are used by companies for specialized tasks or, more frequently, for adding staff during periods of high demand.

Immigration and Reform Act of 1996 This federal law makes it unlawful to hire knowingly an illegal alien, typically someone who has the wrong papers or non at all.

induction Employer use this process to acquaint new employees to the company, his job responsibilities and to his fellow workers.

J

job description Companies use these documents to formally describe the duties, functions, title, authority and responsibilities of a particular job.

job enrichment This is an attempt to redesign jobs (usually to make them more interesting or more challenging) to motivate people to work to their full capacity and ability, and improve employee morale, job satisfaction and commitment to the organization.

job posting Internal recruiting that publicizes open job positions in a company to its current employees via the company bulletin board, company newsletter, internal email, or a combination of these. This kind of recruiting has the advantage of making employees feel that there are opportunities for advancement within their own company, thereby motivating them and accordingly reducing turnover. It has the disadvantage of making companies more inclusive by failing to bring in new employees who may bring fresh ideas and innovation to the company.

M

mentoring This practice pairs new employees with more experienced colleagues in order to make an easy and productive transition to the new company.

merit pay This is typically financial compensation in addition to a worker's salary as a reward for above average job performance, e.g. year-end bonus.

N

new employee orientation The planned introduction of new members of a team to their jobs, coworkers and the policies and expectations of the company for which they will be working.

noncompete agreements An employer who employs an individual with particular skills, training, or knowledge (or an employee who gains specialist knowledge by working for the employer) may ask that employee to sign an agreement stating that, if that employee leaves the company, the employee will not work for a competitor for a specified period of time. Noncompete agreements that attempt to prevent an employee from future work in his profession are usually nonenforceable for the reason that courts view them as unreasonable.

O

online recruitment Employers or private firms use the Internet to post job vacancies and the specifics about the job and how to apply for it.

on-the-job training (OJT) Assigning employment trainees to particular jobs and asking them to observe and learn from supervisors or employees already doing those jobs. This is the most widely used form of training in the United States. Its advantages are its low cost and the opportunities it provides for interaction between trained employees and newcomers. Its disadvantage is that some employees are reluctant to take time away from their own job to help a new employee.

open-ended interview This kind of employment interview encourages the candidate to talk freely and at length about the topics introduced by the interviewer.

P

Pregnancy Discrimination Act (PDA) of 1978 An amendment to Title VII of the Civil Rights Act of 1964 that states that sexual discrimination also includes discrimination as a result of pregnancy and childbirth. In effect, women cannot be subjected to adverse treatment because of pregnancy.

progress discipline This is a corrective action taken by employers when an employee does not meet work standards or has violated company work rules or policies, e.g. being late for work.

professional development A process aimed at assisting and encouraging individuals to improve their job performance and potential by developing their knowledge, skills, abilities, and values. Also, the process of keeping current in one's occupation or profession, remaining open to new ideas and approaches.

R

recruitment Generally this is the process to ensure that an employer has qualified candidates for open positions within the company.

S

selection criteria These are the ideal characteristics that if possessed by a person to a minimal degree would ensure successful performance of a given job.

selection interview This is a structured process whereby the interviewer attempts to learn about a candidate's opinions, beliefs and attitudes and to get to know the candidate as an individual.

sexual harassment There are two kinds in the workplace, both not allowed by law: Quid pro quo (submission to a supervisor's advances) and hostile environment.

U

U.S. Training and Employment Service This federal agency supervises state employment agencies which provide services to people who are without employment and are seeking employment.

Appendix II
Best Practices When Hiring New Employees

Recruiting and Hiring the Right Way

While this book is all about the creative and innovative ways to recruit and hire top talent, all hiring decisions must be made legally and ethically-objectively and free of bias. The law requires it and it is simply good business. Furthermore, hiring new employees works best when the company has taken the time to write job descriptions and created an employee manual which clearly outlines company policies and expectations.

The material that follows is designed to give you a quick overview of best practice in these three areas. While there is much more to be said on all these subjects, the basics are summarized to help you in the all important task of networking and hiring quality employees.

Employment Law

Know the Laws
There are general guidelines to follow when hiring employees, whether your organization is large or small. You want to ensure that prospective employees can do their jobs and adapt to the culture and environment in which they will work. You also want to ensure that you abide by all applicable state and federal laws. The following federal laws are important for all who participate in the interview and selection process.

Equal Pay Act of 1963

This law prohibits wage discrimination by requiring equal pay for equal work. Equal work is defined by four elements:

- Equal skills: The experience, training, education and ability required to perform a job.
- Equal effort: The physical or mental exertion needed to perform a job.
- Equal responsibility: The extent to which an employer relies on an employee to perform the job as expected, with an emphasis on accountability.
- Equal working conditions: The physical surroundings and any job hazards, including inside or outside work, excessive heat or cold, and the quality of workplace ventilation.

There are exceptions to this law, including:

- a seniority system
- a merit pay system
- geographic wage differentials
- a real difference in the quality or quantity of expected work output

Immigration Reform and Control Act of 1986

This law prohibits discrimination against applicants on the basis of national origin or citizenship; establishes penalties for hiring illegal aliens; and requires employers to establish each employee's identity and eligibility to work.

Under this law, when hiring, employers with four or more employees may not:

- Discriminate because of national origin against U.S. citizens, U.S. nationals or authorized aliens.
- Discriminate because of citizenship status against U.S. citizens, U.S. nationals, or aliens in the following classes who have work authorizations: Permanent residents, temporary residents (i.e., individuals who have gone through the legalization program), refugees, and those seeking asylum.

Employers comply with the law by following the verification requirements on Form I-9, which include:

- Hiring only those individuals who are legally authorized to work in the United States. A U.S. citizen-only hiring policy is generally illegal. However, U.S. citizenship may be a requirement for certain jobs under federal, state or local law, or by government contract.

- Completing Form I-9 for all new hires. This form helps employers establish that their employees are legally authorized to work in the United States.
- Allowing new hires to present any document or combination of documents to confirm their identity and/or employment eligibility. Employers cannot prefer one document over another for purposes of completing the form, because not all authorized aliens carry the same documents. Any documents that are allowed by law and that appear to be genuine should be accepted.

Title VII of the Civil Rights Act of 1964

Title VII prohibits discrimination based on race, color, religion, sex, or national origin. The law transformed American society by outlawing discrimination in public facilities, in government and in employment. According to the law:

> It shall be an unlawful employment practice for an employer…to fail or refuse to hire or to discharge any individual, or otherwise to discriminate against any individual with respect to his compensation, terms, conditions, or privileges of employment, because of such individual's race, color, religion, sex, or national origin….

Title VII governs both the hiring process and the duration of employment. This law sets the stage for additional topics covered in later chapters.

Americans with Disabilities Act of 1990 (ADA)

This law prohibits employment discrimination against qualified individuals with disabilities. A qualified individual possesses the skills, experience and education to perform the essential functions of a job, with or without reasonable accommodation.

To be protected under the ADA, an individual must:

- Have a physical or mental impairment that substantially limits one or more major life activities;
- have a record of such an impairment; and
- be regarded as having such an impairment.

Major life activities are those essentials such as:

- Bathing–the ability to wash oneself.
- Dressing–the ability to dress oneself and attach braces, artificial limbs or devices.
- Toileting–the ability to get to and on and off the toilet and maintaining hygiene.
- Transferring–the ability to get in and out of a chair or bed without equipment.
- Continence–the ability to control elimination functions.
- Eating–the ability to get nourishment.
- Learning–the ability to learn.

An essential function is a primary job duty that a qualified individual must be able to perform. It may be considered essential either because it is a key job requirement or because it is highly specialized. A reasonable accommodation is the modification of a job or a work environment that enables a qualified individual with a disability to perform the job's essential functions.

Employers covered by the ADA must ensure that qualified individuals with disabilities:

- Have an equal opportunity to apply for jobs and to work in jobs for which they are qualified;
- have equal access to future promotions;
- have equal access to benefits and privileges of employment, such as employer-provided health insurance or training; and
- are not harassed because of their disability.

An employer covered by the ADA may not ask a job applicant questions as to:

- His or her physical or mental impairment or the origin of that impairment (e.g., why the applicant uses a wheelchair);
- his or her use of medication; and
- his or her history of workers' compensation claims.

An employer covered by the ADA may ask questions as to:

- Whether the applicant has the right education, training and skills for the position;
- whether the applicant can satisfy the job's requirements or essential functions (describe them to the applicant); and

- the amount of time that the applicant was absent when previously employed (but not the reasons for such absences), why the applicant left a previous job, or the nature of any past disciplinary actions.

You may not require a job applicant to have a medical examination until after you have made a conditional job offer. Should the applicant appear to have a disability, however, you may ask whether he or she will need a reasonable accommodation in the workplace, even before you make a conditional job offer.

In summary, questions or comments designed to elicit information regarding an applicant's race, color, ancestry, age, sex, religion, disability or handicap must be avoided in the hiring process.

Job Descriptions

Job Descriptions Define Worker Responsibilities

No matter how large or small your company is, from the CEO on down, everyone in your employment needs a job description. Why are job descriptions so important? Providing a written job description to every employee establishes clear expectations about tasks and responsibilities, and eliminates duplication of effort and finger pointing. In small companies where job functions often overlap, job descriptions provide clear-cut direction to each employee and serve as a benchmark for evaluations, pay increases and bonuses. In larger companies, job descriptions define qualifications and pay scales, and serve as a benchmark for pay increases, bonuses and advancement potential. In any company, job descriptions serve to protect against litigation.

A job description typically outlines the necessary skills, training, and education needed by a potential employee, and lists a job's duties and responsibilities. It can provide a basis for interviewing candidates, orienting a new employee, and evaluating job performance. A well-designed job description simplifies the interview process and informs candidates of a job's requirements. If you know what skills you are looking for, you will have an easier time knowing what questions to ask and identifying which candidates will best fit your open position.

A job description should be reviewed during an employee's performance review to ensure it accurately reflects the job's current duties and responsibilities. Managers should reevaluate job descriptions with their employees, because employees know the work that has been done and that which needs to be done. Human resources professionals should then review the revised description to ensure that it is legally defensible.

Training and development programs help to conform your employees' skills to industry standards. These programs are also used for succession planning or organizational development; for example, what additional skills can an employee acquire to propel the growth of the organization as a whole?

Job descriptions aid in demonstrating compliance with employment laws, most notably the Americans with Disabilities Act (ADA) of 1990. A terminated employee may sue for wrongful discharge. If a company cannot produce even the most basic job description, it will be difficult to prove termination of employment for nonperformance.

Every job description should include the following 15 items:

1. Job title.
2. Job location.
3. Whether the position is exempt or non-exempt according to the Fair Labor Standards Act (FLSA).
4. Financial responsibilities and implications stated in dollars.
5. Summary describing the purpose of the job and why it exists.
6. Listing of specific duties and major responsibilities, especially the essential duties of the job. A task is considered essential if the job exists in order to perform the function. There are is a limited number of people who can perform the duties of a job, and failure to do so can adversely effect the organization. A good way to determine responsibilities is to estimate the number of hours spent in performing a function within a 40-hour week. Estimate a percentage of time each task will take to complete; all percentages should add to 100 percent.
7. Job qualifications, describing the minimum education, experience, and skills necessary to perform the job. Examples: Conditions of employment such as lifting amount in pounds; frequency of bending, stair climbing, kneeling, twisting; environmental considerations such as noise exposure, chemicals, dust.

8. Working conditions, describing work-related hazards and environmental conditions that occur while performing the job and the essentials for safety. Examples: The presence of loud noises; the need to remain on one's feet for long stretches of time; or the amount of protective equipment required. Express physical requirements of the job in concrete, quantifiable terms to avoid tagging a job as gender-specific.

9. The ADA established that essential job functions become a legal standard in order to fight discrimination against people of certain physical impairments.

10. A summary statement, including a general statement of duties and mentions to which the employee would report.

11. Job functions, including daily tasks and any supervisory functions. Indicate whether internal and/or external contact is required.

12. Attributes needed for the position. If the position involves the use of machinery or technology, detail the type of machines or technology the position requires. Also detail any technical or educational requirements that may be critical or desired. Provide insight into the type of work environment you want to maintain. Is it purely a business environment, or is the person expected to contribute to the organization's overall spirit.

13. Provide details on the reporting and organizational structure. Include the titles of both the immediate supervisor and any direct reports.

14. Define evaluation criteria.

15. Include the range or grade of compensation rather than a specific figure.

The job description should be free from judgments about how well the job is currently performed or what is expected in the future. It may be used as a tool for measuring and establishing further career development, but these items are better addressed in an employee's performance management plan. Job requirements should be tied directly to job demands. Stay objective and nonjudgmental and never define job specifications with an individual in mind.

Lastly, understand the difference between a job specification and a job description.

- A job specification identifies the skills and abilities needed to perform a job.
- A job description defines the position and describes the job.

Here are eight rules to follow when writing an effective job description:

1. Use clear and concise language.
2. Use nontechnical language whenever possible so that the language is understandable even to a layperson.
3. Avoid unnecessary words.
4. Keep sentence structure as simple as possible. Begin each sentence with an active verb and always use the present tense.
5. Describe the desired outcome of the work.
6. Use generic terms instead of proprietary names.
7. Avoid using gender-based language.
8. Qualify whenever possible.

Descriptions of job titles appear in a variety of forms in the workplace. Recruitment ads, compensation surveys and other benchmarking tools, as well as corporate or departmental development plans all use some method of describing a job.

Creating an Employee Manual

Why Develop an Employee Manual or Handbook?

Generally speaking, all businesses with greater than one employee should develop and implement an employee manual. Some may argue that there is no need for a formal employee manual in a company with fewer than five employees; most experts, however, agree that it is prudent to have a written policy in place regardless of the number of employees. In some states, fair employment and housing laws apply when a company hires its fifth employee. Federal laws governing civil rights, employees with disabilities, and maternity leave apply to companies with a minimum of 15 employees.

Having an employee manual will help prevent you from violating these rules and regulations.

An employee manual or handbook, if done properly, protects both the employee and the employer from potential problems. A well-written employee handbook communicates expectations clearly so that employers and employees operate under the same set of rules. By spelling out the company's policies and procedures that govern employee behavior and company culture, an employee manual helps ensure there will be no misunderstandings, and can significantly decrease the company's chance of being sued. An employee manual provides an employer with a forum to communicate important company standards, benefits, terminology and values.

Having an employee manual also saves time both for you and for your human resources staff. Your employee manual should be a document that your employees refer to on their own instead of repeatedly asking the same questions. Employees typically will not do this on their own; you need to be clear that they are to check with the manual before calling or emailing the human resources department. An employee handbook also helps you train employees well and provides a road map for the company. Your employees will learn more about your company by seeing its policies and philosophies in one place in a way that standard public relations or marketing brochures cannot.

Updating the manual regularly and checking it to make certain it does not contain any inconsistencies or contradictions is critical to its success. The employee handbook plays an essential role in making certain your employees are all treated fairly and consistently. Supervisors need to know that the rules apply to everyone; they cannot treat one employee different from another without running the risk of serious consequences.

Employment manuals should be available in hard copy format that each employee can keep at his or her desk. If the company has sufficient resources, the manual should also be available electronically either online, typically through a company's Intranet or as a word processing document. This is vital information that needs to be readily accessible to everyone in the company.

While selecting the proper content in your manual is absolutely imperative, you also need to choose the tone carefully. The wording of the handbook is crucial. If the handbook is written in a casual style, it might not be taken seriously. If it is written in an academic tone and is too strict or formal, it may be ignored. Sentences that are clear and to the point are less likely to be misinterpreted or misunderstood. Because the manual often provides the employee with their introduction to the company, it needs to be written in a neutral, professional manner. It is helpful to have more than one person proofread the manual. Each person tends to view information just a bit differently from the next; having multiple reviewers go over the manually carefully increases the clarity and comprehension of your handbook.

One danger in developing an employee manual that needs to be considered is the possibility that information will be inadvertently left out or not written clearly. These mistakes should be avoided at all costs as they can drastically increase the chances of litigation. An issue that is addressed incompletely or with room for interpretation can cause major problems for the company. This is why it is critical to be as thorough and complete as possible considering all types of situations. The guidelines below cover general and specific issues to address. You can also use templates put out by established, reputable human resources or law firms to aid you in building the appropriate manual for your company. The manual should always be checked by legal counsel before you distribute it company-wide.

The Challenge

Providing Comprehensive Written Guidelines for Employment

Many manuals begin with a brief history of the company. An introduction can also contain background information about the company as well as the company's philosophy, culture, purpose and goals. Placing a table of contents at the front of the manual is desirable. Many employee manuals also contain an index at the back, but this is optional.

Guidelines for Developing an Effective Employee Manual

Tantamount to creating a comprehensive, effective employee manual is understanding that the employee is entitled to know what is expected of him or her. No one likes to be surprised. Spell out expectations and responsibilities. This is for your benefit as well as your employees. While you need not include every possible situation, you need to be clear concerning the following policies and procedures:

1. Employment policies including an explanation of at-will employment versus contract employment.
2. Attendance policy addressing:
    a. Hours of attendance and work;
    b. flextime policy if available; and
    c. summer hours if applicable.
3. Time off policies, which typically include:
    a. Holidays;
    b. vacations;
    c. sick leave;
    d. personal days;
    e. occasional absence days;
    f. short- and long-term disability;
    g. Family Medical Leave Act (FMLA);
    h. military leave;
    i. jury duty; and
    j. workers' compensation.
4. Compensation and salary structure, including:
    a. The difference between exempt and non-exempt employees;
    b. overtime guidelines; and
    c. comp time guidelines.
5. Employee development and behavior policies, including:
    a. Performance appraisals;
    b. promotions;
    c. disciplinary action;
    d. dress code, both summer and winter;
    e. confidentiality and privacy;
    f. recruitment and employee referrals;
    g. internal applications;
    h. discrimination;
    i. harassment;

Appendix II Best Practices When Hiring New Employees

       j. drug, alcohol, weapon, and workplace violence; and
       k. voice mail, email and Internet communications; and
          building safety.

Policies that focus on specific company benefits should also be spelled out. This can either be within the employee handbook or in a completely separate packet. This information must be updated at least once a year to reflect the new health benefits and pricing structure. These include:

- Health, dental and vision policies;
- life and accident insurance policies;
- flexible spending account policies: this can include day care, health care and commuter spending;
- memorial/life events contribution policies;
- 401(k) or other employee saving plan policies;
- pension plan policies; and
- service awards policies.

When to present the handbook is up to you. Many small companies hand out the manual on an employee's first day. Some larger companies choose to present their employee manual at the time of orientation. They find it valuable to go through the manual with new employees almost page by page so there is no misinterpretation. If you decide to go this route, it is may be more efficient to wait until you have a few employees, but do not wait too long.

Finally, make certain that there is a place in the manual where the employee can indicate that he or she read and understands the stated policies. The employee should either sign and date a hard copy document or send an electronic confirmation. This vital step cannot be overemphasized or ignored. Your employee handbook does no one any good if it is not read. All your research and carefully chosen words will be meaningless if your target audience, namely your employees, do not read what you have written. Also, you can have the most thorough, well-written manual, but if you cannot prove that the employee in question read and accepted your policies, you will have a difficult time defending your case in a court of law.

When you hire an employee, your goal is usually to create and maintain a strong employer-employee relationship. Providing and using a complete, well-written employee manual is an important step in fostering the environment you need to make your employees work hard for you.